Whose Words These Are

Compilation and Commentary by
j. Justin and John J.
Dilenschneider

Published by Significance Press
405 Lexington Avenue – 57th Floor
New York, NY 10174

All verses in this book are public domain or used with the
permission of their respective copyright holders. See
Permissions, pp. 330-331.

ISBN: 978-0-9985289-1-5

DEDICATION

To all artists who strive to carry forth
the English language through rhythm and rhyme.

WHOSE WORDS THESE ARE

CONTENTS

INTRODUCTION

We assembled these poems – and one prose selection – primarily for their memorable lines. Our hope is that readers might not only discover the sources for some of the English language's most famous and oft-quoted statements but also become aware of their contexts. Memorable lines, after all, often encourage further questions: Who said that? or Where's that from? or What's s/he alluding to?

Although some verses in this personal collection may not be considered "poetry" by the academy, many people still quote (or parody) lines from "Trees" or "The House by the Side of the Road." From Middle English verse to mid-twentieth century song, these selections contain frequently-quoted lines, such as "the shot heard round the world," or "the fault...is not in our stars," or "theirs not to reason why," or "the best laid plans of mice and men." Newspaper columnists still reference Yeats' "the centre cannot hold," politicians, Bruce Springsteen and sportscasters will often revisit Dylan Thomas' "do not go gently into that good night," and even a recent U.S. Supreme Court opinion alluded to Bob Dylan's "the times they are a-changin'." Thus, even today, these memorable lines and verses continue directing us, both linguistically and philosophically, to what distinguished professors George Lakoff and Mark Johnson referred to in 1980 as the everyday "metaphors we live by."

For the most part, as the selections are arranged chronologically, they illustrate the development of the English language. Despite this collection's historical arrangement, we hope that readers will feel free to dip into the book wherever they please, being aided by the index of memorable lines or the index of authors.

Fully aware of today's ever-present, information-ladened "tyranny of the urgent," we seek to encourage (rather than discourage) reading. To that end, we have purposely selected short passages for our readers. We also hope some of these works will be memorized in full, understanding that committing these poems, or at least significant portions of them, to memory will not only help readers to enlarge their present vocabularies but also enable them to absorb the rhythm, rhyme and overall cadence of English — a particular benefit, we think, to persons being introduced to the language. After all, voiced rhyme and rhythm are the universally-shared attributes of both verse and song – and often much goodwill – around the world. Moreover, we believe good reading, reciting and recalling leads to good writing in general. Those who read well will come to write well, think well, and communicate well.

Though we conclude with a fifty-year-old piece from Bob Dylan (not necessarily a bad finalé), we furthermore acknowledge modern poetry and both the subsequent re-surfacing of verse-orality and today's ever-evolving, rhythmically-driven, oral contributions through emergent vehicles, such as hip-hop, rap, air pop, EDM, and other progressive genres. This compilation, along with its commentary, however, attempts to elevate both past rhythmic verse and memorable lines that continue to echo within mainstream culture today. Concomitantly, we endeavor also to reveal how historical iambic-metering still serves as solid, rhythmic footing for much of the modern verse we hear and speak early in the twenty-first century.

With future, even now-being-made memorable lines sure to come, and most assuredly confident that we have successfully over-or-underrepresented every gender, generation, ethnic-group, class, and international contribution to the English language, we have stated our objectives. We think others too may share similar concerns regarding the decline in writing ability, the inability to recognize the English language's important quotes and allusions, and the general lack of an understood overview of English literature. However unsupported by any research, we think our goals have a certain "truthiness" about them, so let us begin.

j. Justin and John J. Dilenschneider

WHOSE WORDS THESE ARE

INDEX OF MEMORABLE LINES

Whose Words These Are

Notes for *Canterbury Tales*

* Line 3 **vein** = roots of plants
* Line 5 **zepherus** = west wind

This fragment of eighteen lines (with modern English interlineated) is part of the 850-plus line general prologue to *The Canterbury Tales* written by Geoffrey Chaucer. Chaucer conceived the *The Canterbury Tales* as stories a group of pilgrims would tell each other to pass the time as they travelled in the spring on a journey (pilgrimage) to the town of Canterbury (where St. Thomas Becket is buried). When he began writing *The Canterbury Tales* in 1386, Chaucer had intended that each of thirty pilgrims would tell four stories, two on the way to Canterbury and two on the return. In addition, he had planned to include accounts of the trip, activities at Canterbury, and a concluding final banquet for the person who told the best story. Chaucer, however, was unable to complete his ambitious undertaking before his death in 1400, and so we have only twenty-four tales and some fragments. Because of the pilgrims' diverse backgrounds and varying occupations, some of the stories are very funny, some are sad, and some try to narrate a moral lesson.

This particular version of the Prologue is taken from the first printed edition by William Caxton in 1476.

Chaucer wrote in a language now called "Middle English," spanning the period of 1066~1485 CE. He is considered the poet who most adeptly merged poetic devices from the "Old English" (some call this era "Early English") period, 449~1066 CE, namely alliteration: the commencement of two or more stressed syllables of a word group either with the same consonant sound or sound group, as in 'from *st*em to *st*ern,' and rhyme. Rhyme was Chaucer's primary poetic device, as evidenced in this general prologue fragment, and rhyme then became the first and favored poetic device from the "Middle English" period onward.

"When April with its showers sweet...."

Canterbury Tales
Prologue

*1. **Whan that Apprill with his shouris sote***
When April with its showers sweet

*2. **And the droghte of marche hath percid p' rote,***
Has pierced the dryness of March to the root,

*3. **And bathid every veyne in suche licour*** *
And bathed every vein in such liquid

*4. **Of whiche vertue engendrid is the flour;***
By which power the flower is created;

*5. **Whanne zepherus eke with his sote breth****
When zepherus also with its sweet breath,

*6. **Enspirid hath in every holt and heth***
Has breathed life into every wood and field

*7. **The tendir croppis, and the yong sonne***
(And) the tender new leaves; and the young sun

*8. **Hath in the ram half his cours y ronne,***
Has run half its course in the ram (in Aries),

*9. **And smale foulis make melodie,***
And small birds make melody,

*10. **That sleppn al nyght with open ye***
Those that sleep all the night with open eyes

*11. **(So prikith hem nature in her corage),***
(So nature propels them in their hearts),

Notes for *Canterbury Tales* (cont.)

* Line 13 **palmers** = "pilgrims who wander"
* Line 14 **foreign halls** = distant shrines
        sundry = various
* Line 17 **holy blessed martyr** = Saint Thomas a' Becket

English poetry is roughly demarcated into the following four, general eras, with more specifically-demarcated periods (as one would expect given the growing amount of writing and developing scholarship) during both the "Early Modern" and "Present-day" eras:

Old English (*Anglo-Saxon Period*)	**449~1066 CE**
Middle English (*Medieval English*)	**1066~1485**
Early Modern English	**1485~1800**
Present-day English	**1800~present**

For a detailed explanation of the differences between BC and BCE; AD and CE, see the first paragraph on page 66 in this collection.

Geoffrey Chaucer (c. 1343~October 25, 1400), is called the "Father of English Literature" because he wrote in English when most of the literature in England was written in French and/or Latin. He is usually considered both the greatest English poet of the Middle Ages and, along with John Milton and William Shakespeare, one of the three great English poets. Speaking English, Latin, French and Italian, Chaucer had an active career in the civil service as a bureaucrat, diplomat, comptroller in the Port of London, clerk of the King's works, and was the first poet of many to have been buried in the "Poets' Corner" of Westminster Abbey. Among his many poems were the "House of Fame," "Troilus and Criseyde," and *The Canterbury Tales,* for which he is best known.

12. **Than longyng folk to gon on pilgrimage,**
Then people long to go on pilgrimages,

13. **And palmers for to seke straunge strondis,***
And itinerant pilgrims to seek foreign shores,

14. **To ferne holollies, cowthe in sondry londis;***
To foreign halls, known in sundry lands;

15. **And specially fro every shiris ende**
And specially from every shire's end

16. **Of yngelond to Cauntirbury thy wende,**
Of England to Canterbury they travel,

17. **The holy blissful martir for to seke,***
To seek the holy blessed martyr,

18. **That them hath holpyn whan they were seke.**
Who helped them when they were sick.

Geoffrey Chaucer

Notes for **"Vision of Piers Plowman"**

This prologue to "The Vision of Piers Plowman" begins in the Malvern Hills, Worcestershire when the wandering poet falls asleep. When the poem continues after this prologue, the poet has a vision of a tower set high upon a hill and a fortress (*dongeon*) lying deep in a valley. The tower is a symbol of Heaven and the "dungeon" is a symbol of Hell. Between these two symbolic places, there is a "fair field full of folk," representing the world of mankind. In the early part of the poem, Piers, the humble plowman of the title, appears and offers himself as the poet's guide to truth. The later part of the work is concerned with the poet's search for Dowel, ("Do-Well") Dobet ("Do-Better") and Dobest ("Do-best"), three persons who, as their names suggest, illustrate the ways of virtue. In particular, Dowel illustrates the virtue of conscience, Dobet the virtue of grace, and Dobest the virtue of charity.

Considered a poem written in Middle English "The Vision of Piers Plowman," written between 1350 and 1387, makes extensive use of the device of **alliteration** (the occurrence of the same consonant or sound at the beginning of adjacent or closely connected words). Alliteration was often used six hundred years earlier by poets, who wrote what we now call Early English. The most famous of these Early English poems is *Beowulf*, written by an unknown poet around the year 700 BCE.

The English poet **William Langland** (c.1332~c.1400) was probably born at Ledbury in Herefordshire. He earned a poor living by singing in a chantry and by copying legal documents. He lived many years in London in poverty. Unlike Geoffrey Chaucer, who wrote at the same time about knights and lords and ladies and priests, Langland wrote about the serfs and herdsmen. His poem "The Vision of Piers Plowman" tells about the conditions of the poor in the 14th century.

"I went through this world to witness wonders."

Vision of Piers Plowman
(Prologue)

In a somer seson, whan softe was the sonne,
In a summer season when the sun was soft,
I shoop me into shroudes as I a sheep were,
Shrouded in a smock in shepherd's clothing,
In habite as an heremite unholy of werkes,*
In the habit of a hermit without good works,
Wente wide in this world wondres to here.
I went through this world to witness wonders.
On a May morwenynge on Malverne hilles
On a May morning on a Malvern hillside
Me bifel a ferly, of Fairye me thoghte.
I saw strange sights like scenes of a Fairy.
I was wery forwandred and wente me to reste
I was weary of wandering and went to rest
Under a brood bank by a bourne syde;
By the bank of a brook in a broad meadow;
And as I lay and lenede and loked on the watres,
As I lay and leaned and looked on the water,
I slombred into a slepyng, it sweyed so murye.
I slumbered and slept so sweetly it murmured.
Thanne gan I meten a merveillous swevene–
Then I met with marvelous visions –

William Langland

***Line 3 – "…hermite unholy of workes,"** = some hermits took alms (gifts, donations, charity) from the people but did not do good works. The poet implies he has not done good works and learns that faith without good works does not lead to heaven.

Notes for **"The Passionate Shepherd to His Love"**

"The Passionate Shepherd to His Love" is one of the most famous English love poems. It was probably written in 1593 but not published until 1599 after Marlowe's death. It is known for its philosophy of "carpe diem" (Latin for *seize the day*, meaning enjoy life now because tomorrow is uncertain).

The poem is written in quatrains (four line stanzas); each line in iambic tetrameter. An "iamb" is a two-syllable measure, sometimes called a 'foot' or 'meter,' with the second syllable accented (sounds like = *da dum*); tetrameter means four measures (tetra = four, meter = measures). Thus, each line has four beats — or four measures:

"da dum, da dum, da dum, da dum."

Writing during the same time as Christopher Marlowe (1564~1593) were the playwrights William Shakespeare (1564~1616) and Ben Jonson (1573~1637). And writing in Spain and dying on the same date as Shakespeare, April 23, 1616 (but not the same day) was Miguel de Cervantes (1547~1616). Among other writers of the time were the poet John Donne, who wrote "No Man is an Island," Edmund Spenser (1522~1599), the author of the long beautiful allegorical poem "The Faerie Queen," the poet and statesman Sir Walter Raleigh (1552~1618), and the lawyer and essayist Francis Bacon (1561~1626) who was Lord Chancellor of England under King James I.

Christopher Marlowe (1564~1593) is considered to be the greatest English playwright before Shakespeare. His major plays were *Edward II, The Jew of Malta, The Tragical History of Dr. Faustus* and *Tamburlaine*. There is also some evidence that he may have helped Shakespeare crafting and writing his earlier plays *Titus Andronicus* and *Richard III*. Marlowe was also a great lyric poet known for his love poems. Unlike Shakespeare, Marlowe was university educated, receiving a B.A. and an M.A. from Benet College. He lived a boisterous life and died in a tavern during a fight about a bill for ale and supper.

To understand the historical and etymological differences between play**wright**, play**write** (not a word), and play**writing**, google 'playwright or playwrite?' and discover the difference.

"Come live with me and be my love,...."

The Passionate Shepherd to His Love

Come live with me and be my love,
And we will all the pleasures prove
That valleys, groves, hills, and fields,
Woods, or steepy mountain yields.

And we will sit upon the rocks,
Seeing the shepherds feed their flocks,
By shallow rivers to whose falls
Melodious birds sing madrigals.

And I will make thee beds of roses
And a thousand fragrant posies,
A cap of flowers, and a kirtle
Embroidered all with leaves of myrtle;

A gown made of the finest wool
Which from our pretty lambs we pull;
Fair lined slippers for the cold,
With buckles of the purest gold;

A belt of straw and ivy buds,
With coral clasps and amber studs;
And if these pleasures may thee move,
Come live with me, and be my love.

The shepherds' swains shall dance and sing
For thy delight each May-morning:
If these delights thy mind may move,
Then live with me and be my love.

Christopher Marlowe

Notes for **"The Nymph's Reply to the Shepherd"**

Philomel = (or ***Philomela***) In Greek mythology, she was one of Pandion's two daughters who were both turned into birds. According to Greek legend, Philomela was rendered into a swallow; her sister Procne – a nightingale. Roman myth-writers reversed these bird types. To understand Raleigh's allusion in the third line of the second stanza, read the Greek myth to see how Philomel(a) becomes 'dumb' by having her tongue cut out by her brother-in-law.

Sir Walter Raleigh wrote this poem in 1600, a year after the publication of Christopher Marlow's poem "The Passionate Shepherd to his Love" (on the previous page here). Answering Marlowe's poem, Raleigh suggests, because in time everything changes, the life that Marlowe's shepherd proposes to his love is not real. Now read Marlowe's second stanza, note his birds, and then compare Raleigh's stanza-by-stanza critique to the very end.

Imitating the rhythm of Marlowe's poem, Raleigh's poem is also written in quatrains (four line stanzas) each line in iambic tetrameter, with a rhyme scheme of **aabb ccdd eeff gghh iibb jjbb** — note the slight word-meaning variation in the "**bb**" rhyming at both the end of the first stanza and the end of the poem. Finally, like Browning's "My Last Duchess" and Keats' "Endymion" in this collection, there are several examples of 'enjambment' in this poem. For a definition of 'enjambment' refer to the final paragraph on p. 204.

Sir Walter Raleigh (1552~1618) was one of the great writers living at the time of Queen Elizabeth. He was also a soldier, a spy, and an explorer, having brought tobacco back from the New World. Raleigh explored different parts of South America, writing a book that gave rise to the legend of El Dorado, and he also assisted the poet Edmund Spencer (1522~1599) publish his epic poem, *The Faerie Queen*. During Raleigh's life he was in and out of favor in the Court of Queen Elizabeth I. Raleigh was executed during the reign of James I on a charge of treason, which was probably false. As courteous a man as Raleigh was known to be, a famous legend notes that he once put his cloak over a puddle so Queen Elizabeth would not get her feet wet when crossing it.

"But could youth last, and love still breed,…."

The Nymph's Reply to the Shepherd

If all the world and love were young,
And truth in every Shepherd's tongue,
These pretty pleasures might me move,
To live with thee, and be thy love.

Time drives the flocks from field to fold,
When Rivers rage and Rocks grow cold,
And Philomel becometh dumb,
The rest complains of cares to come.

The flowers do fade, and wanton fields,
To wayward winter reckoning yields,
A honey tongue, a heart of gall,
Is fancy's spring, but sorrow's fall.

Thy gowns, thy shoes, thy beds of Roses,
Thy cap, thy kirtle, and thy posies
Soon break, soon wither, soon forgotten:
In folly ripe, in reason rotten.

Thy belt of straw and Ivy buds,
The Coral clasps and amber studs,
All these in me no means can move
To come to thee and be thy love.

But could youth last, and love still breed,
Had joys no date, nor age no need,
Then these delights my mind might move
To live with thee, and be thy love.

Sir Walter Raleigh

Notes for **Richard III**, Act 1; Scene 1

The first words of Shakespeare's play, *Richard III*: "Now is the winter of our discontent" are probably the most misquoted of all of Shakespeare's lines. Those who have not read the play, or even the first few lines, erroneously use the phrase to refer to the present time as being unpleasant. For example, in the January 31st, 2014 issue of *The Wall Street Journal,* an article about the simultaneous extreme cold and unusual warmth across the United States was captioned "Now is the Winter of Our Discontent."

But the meaning is just the opposite. "Now" refers to the present time being (figuratively) glorious summer. An accurate reading of these first few lines reveals, in this opening soliloquy, Gloucester (who is later to become Richard III) contemplating the ascendency of his elder brother, Edward IV to the throne of England in place of Henry VI. "The winter of our discontent…," says Gloucester, is "now …made glorious summer by this "sun of York" (sun is a pun on the word 'son'; both Edward and Gloucester were sons of the Duke of York). The winter has passed. The summer is now. The clouds on the House of York are lifted says Gloucester and the battles are over. Instead of fighting, my brother now "capers nimbly" in a lady's chamber to the music of a lute.

Continuing his soliloquy, Gloucester further contemplates his own deformity (once considered humpbacked, but the recent discovery of Richard III's bones has revealed a severe curvature of the spine) and tells of his plans to take the throne.

At the end of the play, Gloucester (now Richard III) is challenged at the Battle of Bosworth Field. At the climax of the battle, Richard, who reputedly was known to be a great warrior when mounted but, because of his scoliosis, was vulnerable when dismounted, is unhorsed. Thus, in another famous line from the play, and just before he dies, Richard cries out:

"A horse! A horse! My kingdom for a horse!"

"Now is the winter of our discontent
Made glorious summer by this sun of York;...."

from *Richard III*,
Act 1; Scene 1

Enter GLOUCESTER:

Now is the winter of our discontent
Made glorious summer by this sun of York;
And all the clouds that lour'd upon our house
In the deep bosom of the ocean buried.
Now are our brows bound with victorious wreaths;
Our bruised arms hung up for monuments;
Our stern alarums changed to merry meetings,
Our dreadful marches to delightful measures.
Grim-visaged war hath smooth'd his wrinkled front;
And now, instead of mounting barded steeds
To fright the souls of fearful adversaries,
He capers nimbly in a lady's chamber
To the lascivious pleasing of a lute.
But I, that am not shaped for sportive tricks,
Nor made to court an amorous looking-glass;
I, that am rudely stamp'd, and want love's majesty
To strut before a wanton ambling nymph;
I, that am curtail'd of this fair proportion,
Cheated of feature by dissembling nature,
Deformed, unfinish'd, sent before my time
Into this breathing world, scarce half made up,
And that so lamely and unfashionable
That dogs bark at me as I halt by them;
Why, I, in this weak piping time of peace,
Have no delight to pass away the time,

Notes for **Richard III**, Act 1; Scene 1 (cont.)

William Shakespeare (1564~1616), an English poet and dramatist, is the most famous author in all of English literature.

William Shakespeare was born and died in Stratford-upon-Avon, England but spent most of his life in London. Like many of his contemporaries, Shakespeare wrote poetry, and his collection of Sonnets is very well known. But his fame rests mostly upon both the thirty-seven plays he is credited with writing and many others he may have had a hand in creating. His earliest plays were the three about *Henry VI* in 1590. During the next six years he wrote nine plays including *Richard III, King John, The Taming of the Shrew* and *A Midsummer Night's Dream.* In 1596, when he wrote *The Merchant of Venice,* he also wrote *Romeo and Juliet* and followed this with *Henry IV (parts I and II)* and *Henry V.* Then from 1597 to 1598 he wrote *Much Ado About Nothing, As You Like It* and *Twelfth Night.* In the next seven years, from 1599 to 1606, he wrote *Julius Caesar, Hamlet, Othello, King Lear,* and *Macbeth.* Between 1607 and 1612 he wrote nine plays concluding with the *The Tempest.*

Shakespeare is known not only for this prolific output of verse but also for both his plays' well-developed characters and the beauty of his language's overall humanity, wisdom, and wit.

Unless to spy my shadow in the sun
And descant on mine own deformity:
And therefore, since I cannot prove a lover,
To entertain these fair well-spoken days,
I am determined to prove a villain
And hate the idle pleasures of these days.
Plots have I laid, inductions dangerous,
By drunken prophecies, libels and dreams,
To set my brother Clarence and the king
In deadly hate the one against the other:
And if King Edward be as true and just
As I am subtle, false and treacherous,
This day should Clarence closely be mew'd up,
About a prophecy, which says that 'G'
Of Edward's heirs the murderer shall be.
Dive, thoughts, down to my soul: here
Clarence comes.

William Shakespeare

Notes for the **Prologue** to *Romeo and Juliet*

In a sonnet spoken by the Chorus, these are the opening lines of William Shakespeare's play *Romeo and Juliet* that set out the entire plot of the play. The Montague and Capulet families have quarreled for many years and, as the sonnet implies, "their parents' rage, / Which, but their children's end (i.e., death), nought could remove,...."

Note the tidiness, straightforwardness, direction, and audience acknowledgement of the prologue's summary of the soon-to-come performance. It contains the same kind of introductory background information (time, place and actors) and thesis needed when writing in most forms of English composition.

In addition, notice how the alternate line, rhyme-scheme allows the sonnet to "flow," ending with Shakespeare's traditional rhymed couplet.

William Shakespeare (1564~1616), an English poet and dramatist, is the most famous author in all of English literature. He was born and died in Stratford-upon-Avon, England, but spent most of his adult life in London. Like many of his contemporaries, Shakespeare wrote poetry, and his collection of sonnets is also very well known. But his fame rests mostly upon the thirty-seven plays he is credited with writing and many others he may have had a hand in creating.

"...star-cross'd lovers...."

from *Romeo and Juliet*
Prologue

Two households, both alike in dignity,
In fair Verona, where we lay our scene,
From ancient grudge break to new mutiny,
Where civil blood makes civil hands unclean.
From forth the fatal loins of these two foes
A pair of star-cross'd lovers take their life;
Whose misadventured piteous overthrows
Do with their death bury their parents' strife.
The fearful passage of their death-mark'd love,
And the continuance of their parents' rage,
Which, but their children's end, nought could remove,
Is now the two hours' traffic of our stage;
The which if you with patient ears attend,
What here shall miss, our toil shall strive to mend.

William Shakespeare

Notes for *The Merchant of Venice,* Act 4; Scene 1

* **strained** = not constrained or held back
* **It** = refers to "mercy" throughout the speech
* **twice blest** = bestows a double blessing
* **shows** = represents
* **dread** = reverence/awe
* **above** = more than
* **sceptred sway** = royal government/ kingly power
* **likest** = most like
* **seasons** = modifies
  Jew = Shylock
* **same prayer** = Lord's Prayer/ "Our Father" in which we
  pray for mercy "forgive us our trespasses"
  render = perform in return/ *"forgive us our trespasses*
  as we forgive those ..."
* **To mitigate** = to ask you to modify your request for
  justice by being merciful

Written in iambic pentameter and spoken by Portia who, at the time, is disguised as a judge, this is one of the most quoted speeches from all of Shakespeare's plays. After saying how important mercy is, and how we are most like God when we are merciful, toward the end of the speech Portia asks Shylock to consider this: if there was only justice, and not mercy, none of us would go to heaven.

The Merchant of Venice has often been called an anti-Semitic play because the antagonist Shylock, a money-lender who seems to seek compensatory revenge, is Jewish and is referred to as "the Jew." Because Jewish people were barred from England from 1290 to 1660, it is doubtful that Shakespeare ever met a Jewish person, just as it is highly unlikely he was ever in Venice. That a great writer such as Shakespeare could adopt the stereotype of the time concerning the Jewish people should cause readers to examine their own prejudices.

Finally, the phrase **"a pound of flesh"** is still both often heard in the world of business/commerce and in the field of economics.

"The quality of mercy is not strained;…"

from *The Merchant of Venice*
Act 4; Scene 1: lines 184~202
(Portia's speech to Shylock about mercy)

*In **The Merchant of Venice**, Shylock bargained
for a pound of Antonio's flesh if Antonio failed to pay
back a loan. Antonio could not pay. Shylock now
wants his **pound of flesh**. Portia (the heroine of
the play disguised as a judge) asks him to be merciful.*

The quality of mercy is not strained;*
It droppeth as the gentle rain from heaven*
Upon the place beneath. It is twice blest;*
It blesseth him that gives and him that takes:
'Tis mightiest in the mightiest; it becomes
The throned monarch better than his crown:
His sceptre shows the force of temporal power,*
The attribute to awe and majesty,
Wherein doth sit the dread and fear of kings;*
But mercy is above this sceptred sway;*
It is enthronèd in the hearts of kings,
It is an attribute to God himself;
And earthly power doth then show likest God's*
When mercy seasons justice. Therefore, Jew,*
Though justice be thy plea, consider this,
That, in the course of justice, none of us
Should see salvation: we do pray for mercy;
And that same prayer doth teach us all to render*
The deeds of mercy. I have spoke thus much
To mitigate the justice of thy plea;*
Which if thou follow, this strict court of Venice
Must needs give sentence 'gainst the merchant there.

William Shakespeare

Notes for *Henry V*, Act 4; Scene 3

In 1415, during the middle period of the Hundred Years War, the British under Henry V invaded France. After they took Harfleur in September and had moved through eastern Normandy, they crossed the Somme and were heading northward when intercepted by a large French force led by the constable Charles I d'Albret.

Vastly outnumbered, the British were forced to fight on a plain within a heavily wooded area known as Agincourt. The French attacked over the sodden open field, which was about 1000 yards wide, and were cut down in a three-hour battle primarily by the British archers. The French lost 1500 knights and 4,500 men-at-arms. British losses were negligible. The Battle of Agincourt was considered the greatest (though not the first) victory for the English longbow.

As an aside, the longbow was capable of firing an arrow over 240 yards. In 1410, Henry IV had reissued Edward III's Act of 1363, making archery practice compulsory for all able-bodied men between the ages of 16 and 60. They were required to practice every Sunday and feast day "...to learn and practice the art of shooting ...whence by God's help may come forth honour to the kingdom and advantage to the king in his actions at war."(Barker, Juliet. 2006. *Agincourt*, Little-Brown: NewYork, p. 88)

Most famous is this speech, which Shakespeare attributed to Henry just before the battle – when his soldiers were both concerned about the odds they were facing and lamenting the fact there were men in England who, because October 25th was a holiday (St. Crispian's Day), "...do no work to-day."

The 25th of October is the feast of Saints Crispin and Crispian, who were brothers born in Rome and who went to Soissons, France in 303 A.D. to spread Christianity, supporting themselves as itinerant shoemakers. The governor of Soissons disapproved of their attempts to make converts to Christianity and had them put to death. The brothers are the patron saints of shoemakers, and in the fifteenth century their feast-day was an occasion for a holiday both in France and in England. Hence, men in England "did no work today."

"We few, we happy few, we band of brothers!"

"All things are ready, if our minds be so."

from *Henry V*
Act 4; Scene 3

***** = omitted lines

EARL OF WESTMORELAND
O that we now had here
But one ten thousand of those men in England
That do no work to-day.

KING HENRY V
What's he that wishes so?
My cousin Westmoreland? No, my fair cousin:
If we are marked to die, we are enow
To do our country loss; and if to live,
The fewer the men the greater share of honour.
God's will! I pray thee, wish not one man more.
*****

Rather proclaim it, Westmoreland, through my host,
That he which hath no stomach to this fight,
Let him depart; his passport shall be made,
And crowns for convoy put in his purse.
We would not die in that man's company
That fears his fellowship to die with us.

Notes for *Henry V*, Act 4; Scene 3 (cont.)

In this speech Henry V tries to unify and inspire the men in his army by telling them that their deeds and those of their comrades will always be remembered.

In this vein, the first memorable line in this speech is

"We few, we happy few, we band of brothers!"

Henry goes on to say that:

For he today that sheds his blood with me
Shall be my brother; be he ne'er so vile,
This day shall gentle his condition;....

In these lines Henry tells his soldiers that a person who fights with him on this day, even if he is from the lower classes ("be he ne'er so vile", that is, even if he is a villain, a person low in birth), he will become a gentleman ("...shall gentle his condition;....").

This day is called the feast of Crispian;
He that outlives this day, and comes safe home,
Will stand a tip-toe when this day is named,
And rouse him at the name of Crispian

He that shall live this day and see old age,
Will yearly on the vigil feast his neighbors,
And say, 'Tomorrow is Saint Crispian.'
Then will he strip his sleeve and show his scars,
And say, 'These wounds I had on Crispin's day.'

Old men forget; yet all shall be forgot,
But he'll remember with advantages
What feats he did that day. Then shall our names,
Familiar in his mouth as household words,
Harry the king, Bedford and Exeter,
Warwick and Talbot, Salisbury and Gloucester,
Be in their flowing cups freshly remembered.

This story shall the good man teach his son;
And Crispin Crispian shall ne'er go by,
From this day to the ending of the world,
But we in it shall be remembered,
We few, we happy few, we band of brothers!

For he today that sheds his blood with me
Shall be my brother, be he ne'er so vile,
This day shall gentle his condition;
And gentlemen in England now a-bed
Shall think themselves accursed that they were not here,
And hold their manhoods cheap whiles any speaks
That fought with us upon Saint Crispin's day.

SALISBURY
My sovereign lord, bestow yourself with speed;
The French are bravely in their battles set,
And will with all expedience charge on us.

Notes for *Henry V*, Act 4; Scene 3 (cont.)

Warned by Salisbury towards the end of his speech that the French are readied in their battle preparations, Henry utters yet another famous line:

"All things are ready if our minds be so."

which brings about a change in heart from his cousin Westmoreland, who at the outset called for reinforcements.

A video version of this complete speech and scene can be found by pasting the following into your Internet browser:

https://www.youtube.com/watch?v=OAvmLDkAgAM
or
www.youtube.com/watch?v=cRj01LShXN8

William Shakespeare wrote this passage in poetic form (in Shakespeare's plays the nobility nearly always speak in poetic verse), in this case iambic pentameter. An iamb is a unit of two syllables - an unstressed syllable followed by a stressed syllable. Pentameter means a measure (meter) of five (penta) units. So there are five iambic units per line. The poet often does vary the lines to avoid monotony.

William Shakespeare (1564~1616) is regarded as the greatest playwright in the English language. Even some four-hundred years after his death, his plays are still produced all over the world.

KING HENRY
All things are ready, if our minds be so.

WESTMORELAND
Perish the man whose mind is backward now!

KING HENRY
Thou dost not wish more help from England, Coz?

WESTMORELAND
God's will! my liege, you and I alone
Without more help, could fight this royal battle!
*****

Enter MONTJOY;
Messenger from the Constable of France

MONTJOY
Once more I come to know of thee, King Harry,
If for thy ransom thou wilt now compound,
Before thy most assured overthrow:
*****

KING HENRY
I pray thee, bear my former answer back:
Bid them achieve me and then sell my bones.
*****

Let me speak proudly: tell the constable
We are but warriors for the working-day;
Our gayness and our gilt are all besmirch'd
*****

But, by the mass, our hearts are in the trim;....
*****

William Shakespeare

Notes for *Julius Caesar*
Act 1; Scene 2

Shakespeare's play *Julius Caesar* is about a group of men led by Brutus and Cassius, who assassinate Julius Caesar on March 15, 44 BCE to prevent him becoming dictator over Rome. The assassins and their followers, pursued by Mark Antony and others loyal to Caesar, are finally killed at the battle of Philippi in October 42 BCE.

Early in the play Cassius tries to convince Brutus to join the band of conspirators who plan to assassinate Caesar. In this scene as well is the Soothsayer's famous forewarning of the tragedy that awaits Caesar: "Beware the ides of March."

In the well-known line, "The fault, dear Brutus, is not in our stars, But in ourselves,..." Cassius tells Brutus that people make their own destiny; that there is no fate that controls their lives. Cassius goes on to convince Brutus that he is just as worthy as Caesar and should join the conspiracy.

William Shakespeare (1564~1616) is perhaps the greatest 'wordsmith' of the English language. With deep insight into the human condition, he wrote so profoundly and prolifically that his words have, and still do, resonate throughout the world on stage, in books, in speeches, in newspaper articles, in song, and in our hearts and minds as we seek to both explain our lives and the everchanging world around us. Indeed, as the stage was Shakespeare's world, we have learned through his words to see and acknowledge the world as our stage.

**"The fault,…, is not in our stars,
But in ourselves,…."**

from *Julius Caesar*
Act 1; Scene 2

***** = lines omitted

*Attempting to persuade him to rebel against Caesar,
Cassius speaks to Brutus*

CASSIUS:

*****

Men at some time are masters of their fates:
The fault, dear Brutus, is not in our stars,
But in ourselves, that we are underlings.
Brutus and Caesar: what should be in that 'Caesar'?
Why should that name be sounded more than yours?
Write them together, yours is as fair a name;
Sound them, it doth become the mouth as well;
Weigh them, it is as heavy; conjure with 'em,
Brutus will start a spirit as soon as Caesar.
*****

William Shakespeare

Notes for *Julius Caesar*
Act 3; Scene 2

This is not a poem, however, we present it as a good illustration of rhetoric, the art of persuasion.

This is a speech by Brutus, who has just assassinated Julius Caesar. Brutus then appears before a crowd of Roman citizens and attempts to justify the assassination of Caesar. After this speech the citizens of Rome are all in favor of Brutus' killing of Caesar. But the next speaker, Mark Antony, changes the minds of the citizens (in this collection, see Antony's speech on p. 33 that begins: "Friends, Romans, Countrymen..."). In this speech, however, which we have taken the liberty to separate into paragraphs, Brutus employs several rhetorical devices to justify his part in killing Caesar:

Paragraph 1: Repeating words or phrases in reverse order. Examples from other time-periods are: "All for one and one for all" (motto of The Three Musketeers), or "Ask not what your country can do for you, but what you can do for your country" (John F. Kennedy's inaugural address). The technical term for this is "**antimetabole**." Note also Brutus' word-play on "censure" and "senses" for an audible reverse repetition.

Paragraph 2: **rhetorical question**, that is, asking a question and then answering it yourself. Often used by politicians today: "Do I believe in climate change? Of course, I do." This device gives the impression that the speaker is in control. Also, by asking questions he can answer, the speaker precludes the audience from asking other questions. In addition, Brutus uses antithesis or contrast: "not loved Caesar less, but loved Rome more."

Paragraph 3: another form of **rhetorical question**, i.e. asking a question in a way that there can be only one answer;

Paragraph 4: **parallelism**: the effective use of successive verbal constructions in poetry or prose that correspond in grammatical structure, sound, meter, and meaning, e.g.

As Caesar loved me, I weep	tears for his love
as he was fortunate, I rejoice	joy for his fortune
as he was valiant, I honour	honour for his valour
	death for his ambition

"If any speak; for him I have offended."

from *Julius Caesar*
Act 3; Scene 2

THIRD CITIZEN:
The noble Brutus is ascended: silence!

BRUTUS:
Be patient till the last. Romans, countrymen, and lovers! hear me for my cause, and be silent, that you may hear: believe me for mine honour, and have respect to mine honour, that you may believe: censure me in your wisdom, and awake your senses,
that you may the better judge.

If there be any in this assembly, any dear friend of Caesar's, to him I say, that Brutus' love to Caesar was no less than his. If then that friend demand why Brutus rose against Caesar, this is my answer: --Not that I loved Caesar less, but that I loved Rome more.

Had you rather Caesar were living and die all slaves, than that Caesar were dead, to live all free men?

As Caesar loved me, I weep for him; as he was fortunate, I rejoice at it; as he was valiant, I honour him: but, as he was ambitious, I slew him. There is tears for his love; joy for his fortune; honour for his valour; and death for his ambition.

Notes for *Julius Caesar* Act 3; Scene 2 (cont.)

Paragraph 5: **a series of parallel rhetorical questions** whereby a person answering would have to admit to being "base," "rude," or "vile."

William Shakespeare (April 23, 1564 [baptized April 26] ~April 23, 1616) was an English actor, poet, and playwright. He wrote thirty-seven plays, 154 sonnets, two long narrative poems and other verses. He is generally considered both the greatest writer in the English language and the greatest dramatist in the world.

Who is here so base that would be a bondman? If any, speak; for him have I offended. Who is here so rude that would not be a Roman? If any, speak; for him have I offended. Who is here so vile that will not love his country? If any, speak; for him have I offended. I pause for a reply.

ALL:
None, Brutus, none.

BRUTUS:
Then none have I offended. I have done no more to Caesar than you shall do to Brutus. The question of his death is enrolled in the Capitol; his glory not extenuated, wherein he was worthy, nor his offences enforced, for which he suffered death.

Enter Antony and others, with Caesar's body
Here comes his body, mourned by Mark Antony: who, though he had no hand in his death, shall receive the benefit of his dying, a place in the commonwealth; as which of you shall not? With this I depart, —that, as I slew my best lover for the good of Rome, I have the same dagger for myself, when it shall please my country to need my death.

ALL:
Live, Brutus! live, live!

William Shakespeare

Notes for Mark Antony's Speech in *Julius Caesar*
Act 3; Scene 2, lines 72~100

This is the beginning of one of the most famous passages in English. It is the turning point of the play *Julius Caesar*. Up to this time in the play the fortunes of Brutus, Cassius, and the rest of the conspirators who killed Julius Caesar have been rising.

At this point Mark Antony speaks to the crowd of citizens immediately after Brutus has spoken and just convinced the people of the justice in assassinating Caesar. When Brutus concludes his speech, the crowd is unanimous in praising him.

Antony then speaks.

Antony starts by assuring the crowd that he does not come to praise Caesar. He then reminds the crowd that Brutus told them that Caesar was ambitious and that Brutus has now given him, Antony, a chance to speak at Caesar's funeral.

This speech is a great example of extended irony (that is, saying what you do not mean). For example, in his speech, Antony, while giving example after example (the passage goes for many more lines) of Caesar's generosity, continually repeats that Brutus is an "honorable man" who says Caesar was "ambitious." Antony's extended irony takes effect, and by the conclusion of the speech, Antony has turned the crowd from praising Brutus to condemning him.

William Shakespeare (1564~1616), is still the greatest of all English authors, and in addition to writing sonnets and poems, he wrote three types of plays: histories, tragedies and comedies (thirty-seven of his own in all). While his written historical dramas were relatively straightforward in their sociohistorical accounting of events, his comedies and histories reveal 'breaks' in the natural order of what was socially (and naturally) acceptable in the day, with outcomes, as you would imagine, being either comedic or tragic.

"Friends, Romans, countrymen, lend me your ears;…"
"For Brutus is an honourable man;…."

from *Julius Caesar*
Act 3; Scene 2, lines 72~100

***** = lines omitted

ANTONY:

Friends, Romans, countrymen, lend me your ears;
I come to bury Caesar, not to praise him.
The evil that men do lives after them;
The good is oft interred with their bones;
So let it be with Caesar. The noble Brutus
Hath told you Caesar was ambitious:
If it were so, it was a grievous fault,
And grievously hath Caesar answer'd it.
Here, under leave of Brutus and the rest—
For Brutus is an honourable man;
So are they all, all honourable men—
Come I to speak in Caesar's funeral.
He was my friend, faithful and just to me:
But Brutus says he was ambitious;
And Brutus is an honourable man.
He hath brought many captives home to Rome
Whose ransoms did the general coffers fill:
Did this in Caesar seem ambitious?
When that the poor have cried, Caesar hath wept:
Ambition should be made of sterner stuff:
Yet Brutus says he was ambitious;
And Brutus is an honourable man.
*****

William Shakespeare

Notes for *Julius Caesar*, Act 4; Scene 3

In this excerpt from Shakespeare's play *Julius Caesar*, Brutus is speaking to a somewhat weary Cassius. Brutus and Cassius and others assassinated Caesar because they thought Caesar would become a dictator, take power, and destroy the Roman republican form of government. After Caesar's assassination, Mark Antony persuaded the citizens of Rome that Brutus and Cassius were traitors to Rome.

The citizens then turned against Brutus and Cassius who fled with their armies.

Mark Antony, Octavius Caesar and Lepidus formed an army and pursued Brutus and Cassius to a place called Philippi. Brutus and Cassius must now decide whether to battle Antony's forces or wait until later. Cassius has just said that he would prefer to wait, however, Brutus is in favor of battle now because his and Cassius' soldiers are ready.

In this famous passage Brutus speaks both about a "...tide in the affairs of men." which can be either "taken at the flood" or "omitted" altogether, and also the consequences of taking one course of action or the other.

(It is interesting to note that serving in Brutus' army was the Roman poet, Horace, whose poem "Happy the Man" is in this collection.)

William Shakespeare (1564~1616) is considered the most widely known and the greatest of all English authors. He wrote many plays and poems.

"There is a tide in the affairs of men,...."

from *Julius Caesar*
Act 4; Scene 3

BRUTUS: (*speaking to Cassius*)

Under your pardon. You must note beside,
That we have tried the utmost of our friends,
Our legions are brim-full, our cause is ripe:
The enemy increaseth every day;
We, at the height, are ready to decline.
There is a tide in the affairs of men,
Which, taken at the flood, leads on to fortune;
Omitted, all the voyage of their life
Is bound in shallows and in miseries.
On such a full sea are we now afloat;
And we must take the current when it serves,
Or lose our ventures.

William Shakespeare

Notes for *Hamlet*, Act 1; Scene 3; lines 540~567

Unfamiliar words and phrases marked with an asterisk:

* **...you are stayed for** = they are holding the ship for you
  my blessing with thee = Polonius gives Laertes his
  blessing
* **character** = write this in your mind
* **unproportioned** = unsuitable/ immoderate
* **familiar** = friendly
* **vulgar** = common
* **adoption tried,** = having been tested
* **dull thy palm** = make your palm callous by shaking
  hands with every man
* **new-hatch'd, unfledg'd** = new/ untested/ untried
* **Bear't that th'** = manage it so that your opponent
* **Give every man thine ear** = listen to everyone
* **censure** = opinion
* **habit** = clothing
* **husbandry** = thrift / prudence with money
* **season** = preserve / help you to remember

This speech occurs early in Shakespeare's tragedy *Hamlet*. Polonius, one of King Claudius's noblemen, is giving advice to his son, Laertes, who is about to depart for France. At the end of the play, Laertes, believing that Hamlet is responsible for both the death of his father, Polonius (which he is), and his sister, Ophelia (which he is not), returns from France and challenges Hamlet to a duel.

Polonius' advice is: (1) don't speak or do anything without first thinking about it; (2) be friendly and love your special friends but you don't have to make everyone special; (3) don't quarrel, but if you do get in an argument, do well; (4) listen to all, but don't make quick judgments; (5) buy clothes you can afford, but not too fancy; (6) don't borrow and don't lend, and most important (7) be yourself.

William Shakespeare (1564~1616), an English poet and dramatist, is the most famous author in all of English literature. He is known not only for his prolific output of poetry plays but also for the beauty, wisdom, and the humanity found in his use of language.

"Above all, to thine own self be true, …."
"Neither a borrower nor a lender be; …."

from *Hamlet*
Act 1; Scene 3: lines 540~567

Polonius' advice to his son Laertes, as Laertes departs for France

Yet here, Laertes? Aboard, aboard, for shame!
The wind sits in the shoulder of your sail,
And you are stay'd for. There- my blessing with thee!*
And these few precepts in thy memory
Look thou character. Give thy thoughts no tongue,*
Nor any unproportion'd thought his act.*
Be thou familiar, but by no means vulgar:*
Those friends thou hast, and their adoption tried,*
Grapple them unto thy soul with hoops of steel;
But do not dull thy palm with entertainment*
Of each new-hatch'd, unfledg'd comrade. Beware*
Of entrance to a quarrel; but being in,
Bear't that th' opposed may beware of thee.*
Give every man thine ear, but few thy voice;*
Take each man's censure, but reserve thy judgment.*
Costly thy habit as thy purse can buy,*
But not express'd in fancy; rich, not gaudy;
For the apparel oft proclaims the man,
And they in France of the best rank and station
Are most select and generous, chief in that.
Neither a borrower nor a lender be;
For loan oft loses both itself and friend,
And borrowing dulls the edge of husbandry.*
This above all: to thine own self be true,
And it must follow, as the night the day,
Thou canst not then be false to any man.
Farewell. My blessing season this in thee!*

William Shakespeare

Notes for *Hamlet* Act 3; Scene 1

Lines with words and phrases marked with an asterisk:

* **To be or not to be** = Hamlet is debating whether or not to put an end to his life
* **slings and arrows** = weapons that we are subjected to by luck or fortune.
* **take arms** = to take up weapons in opposition
* **sea of troubles** = overwhelming multitude (waves) of troubles
* **to sleep** = death as a kind of sleep
* **consummation** = an outcome, a desired goal
* **there's the rub** = there's the difficulty
* **mortal coil** = body bound to earth by a coil (of rope, or chain?)
* **pause** = stop our movement, occasion to reflect or think
* **respect** = consideration, motive
* **contumely** = insolence, rudeness, scorn
* **dispriz'd** = unappreciated
* **the spurns…That patient merit of th' unworthy takes**
= the contempt that a quiet person of merit receives (takes) from unworthy persons.
* **quietus** = a release (a legal term meaning to put a matter at rest)
* **bodkin** = dagger, small knife
* **fardels** = packs, bundles, baggage
* **bourn** = boundary
* **pitch and moment** = important and significant

"To be or not to be, that is the question:...."

"The slings and arrows of outrageous fortune...."

from *Hamlet*

Act 3; Scene 1

HAMLET:

To be, or not to be--that is the question:*
Whether 'tis nobler in the mind to suffer
The slings and arrows of outrageous fortune*
Or to take arms against a sea of troubles*
And by opposing end them. To die, to sleep--*
No more--and by a sleep to say we end
The heartache, and the thousand natural shocks
That flesh is heir to. 'Tis a consummation*
Devoutly to be wished. To die, to sleep--
To sleep--perchance to dream: ay, there's the rub,*
For in that sleep of death what dreams may come
When we have shuffled off this mortal coil,*
Must give us pause. There's the respect*
That makes calamity of so long life.
For who would bear the whips and scorns of time,
Th' oppressor's wrong, the proud man's contumely*
The pangs of dispriz'd love, the law's delay,*
The insolence of office, and the spurns*
That patient merit of th' unworthy takes,
When he himself might his quietus make*
With a bare bodkin? Who would fardels bear,*
To grunt and sweat under a weary life,

Notes for *Hamlet* Act 3; Scene 1 (cont.)

This soliloquy (a talk by oneself, to no particular person) by Hamlet is both perhaps the most quoted of all passages written by Shakespeare and perhaps the most famous passage in all of literature.

Here Hamlet, in the middle of the play, contemplates the pros and cons of suicide.

Earlier in the play (Act 1; Scene 2, lines 129-132) Hamlet, beset by troubles, wishes that God had not ruled against suicide, otherwise he might have taken his own life. In this later soliloquy, where he again talks about taking his own life, his reasons for and against suicide do not consider religion, but rather what should happen to him if there is an after-life.

As it turns out Hamlet decides against suicide, and the play proceeds with stabbings and drownings until its bloody last act, which contains duels and poisonings and invading armies.

William Shakespeare (April 23, 1564 [baptized April 26] ~April 23, 1616) was an English actor, poet, and playwright. He wrote thirty-seven plays, 154 sonnets, two long narrative poems and other verses. He is generally considered to be both the greatest writer in the English language and the greatest dramatist in the world.

But that the dread of something after death,
The undiscovered country, from whose bourn*
No traveller returns, puzzles the will,
And makes us rather bear those ills we have
Than fly to others that we know not of ?
Thus conscience does make cowards of us all,
And thus the native hue of resolution
Is sicklied o'er with the pale cast of thought,
And enterprise of great pitch and moment*
With this regard their currents turn awry
And lose the name of action.

William Shakespeare

Notes for *Macbeth*, Act 5; Scene 5

Here are words spoken by Macbeth near the end of the play. At the play's opening three witches predict that Macbeth would be King of Scotland. To further that prophecy, Macbeth killed Duncan, the then King of Scotland, and became king. Now in Act 5, Macbeth, having learned the English are proceeding against him, receives news that his wife has died and contemplates death. There is a lot packed into these lines.

Macbeth first thinks about how days plod slowly along till the end of "recorded time," meaning, no doubt, time will continue after man is extinct and no longer around to record it. All the past, thinks Macbeth, has only shown ("lighted"= *shown* the way) mortals (fools = mortals. "What "fools" these mortals be." says Puck in *Midsummer Nights' Dream*) the way to their inevitable "dusty" death ("Dust thou are and to dust thou shall return" was God's punishment of Adam for eating of the tree of knowledge. Genesis 3:19).

Macbeth then changes the metaphor and thinks of his life. "Out, out, brief candle!" (the 'candle' being his life. It is time to extinguish the 'candle'). And then he makes the analogy that life is like an actor who, after he acts his role, is gone, never to be heard of again. The play will end. Macbeth finally analogizes a person's life to a 'tale told by and idiot.' It is full of "sound and fury" as we go through it, but in the end, it means nothing.

When the noted Shakespearean actor, Kenneth Branagh, playing the role of Macbeth in 2014, spoke the words, "told by an idiot," he clapped his hands to his head to show he was an idiot for believing the prophecy of the three witches.

The first chapter of the Nobel Prize winning author William Faulkner's 1929 novel *The Sound and Fury* is told by a mentally-challenged man who has difficulty expressing himself. Faulkner knew the intelligent reader would see the connection.

"Tomorrow, and tomorrow, and tomorrow,…"
"…a tale…full of sound and fury,…."

from *Macbeth*
Act 5; Scene 5

***** = lines omitted

MACBETH:

*****

Tomorrow, and tomorrow, and tomorrow,
Creeps in this petty pace from day to day,
To the last syllable of recorded time;
And all our yesterdays have lighted fools
The way to dusty death. Out, out, brief candle!
Life's but a walking shadow, a poor player,
That struts and frets his hour upon the stage,
And then is heard no more. It is a tale
Told by an idiot, full of sound and fury,
Signifying nothing.

William Shakespeare

Notes for *Cymbeline* Act 5; Scene 2

* **the reed is as the oak** = weakness and strength are the same after death.
* **The scepter, learning, physic** = the ruler, the scholar, the   physician

The eminent Shakespearian critic Professor Harold Bloom of Yale University said that this elegy (a funeral lament or song) "could be judged as the finest of all the songs in Shakespeare's plays." He said the play itself, *Cymbeline,* was "uneven" and not even among Shakespeare's best plays. Dr. Samuel Johnson, the eighteenth-century critic, said the play had many pleasing scenes, but he also commented on the "the absurdity of the conduct" in the play.

Spoken in alternating verses by her two brothers, who do not recognize their sister as she is dressed as a boy (one of the absurdities mentioned by Johnson), in Act 4; Scene 2 of the play, these lines, beginning with "Fear no more....," are recited over the body of the main female character, Imogen, who, having drunk a sleeping potion, appears to be dead.

The poem specifically enumerates that which Hamlet generally called "the slings and arrows of outrageous fortune," "the sea of troubles," and "The heartache and the thousand natural shocks that flesh is heir to." But unlike Hamlet's worries about what may come after death, this poem focuses on the rest and quiet and peace and freedom that death will inevitably bring to everyone, to "golden lads," "chimney sweeps," rulers, scholars, doctors and "lovers."

Chimney sweeps often died because dust got into their lungs. Also, "golden lads and girls" return to dust for, as God told Adam when he cast him out of the Garden of Eden, Adam came from dust and as a punishment for his disobedience he, and all his descendants, will return to dust. (Genesis 3:19).

"Fear no more the heat o' the sun,…."

**"Golden lads and girls all must,
As chimney-sweepers, come to dust."**

from *Cymbeline* Act 5; Scene 2

Fear no more the heat o' the sun,
Nor the furious winter's rages;
Thou thy worldly task hast done,
Home art gone, and ta'en thy wages:
Golden lads and girls all must,
As chimney-sweepers, come to dust.

Fear no more the frown o' the great;
Thou art past the tyrant's stroke;
Care no more to clothe and eat;
To thee the reed is as the oak:*
The scepter, learning, physic, must*
All follow this, and come to dust.

Fear no more the lightning flash,
Nor the all-dreaded thunder stone;
Fear not slander, censure rash;
Thou hast finished joy and moan:
All lovers young, all lovers must
Consign to thee, and come to dust.

No exorciser harm thee!
Nor no witchcraft charm thee!
Ghost unlaid forbear thee!
Nothing ill come near thee!
Quiet consummation have;
And renownèd be thy grave!

William Shakespeare

Notes for *The Tempest* Act 4; Scene 1

This speech is given by Prospero, the ruler of an island whose only other residents are his daughter Miranda, a fairy Ariel, and a rebellious servant Caliban. Soonafter, a young noble Ferdinand and his shipmates survive a tempest and become stranded on a remote part of the island. Ferdinand wanders off from his shipmates and meets Miranda, Prospero's daughter. Miranda and Ferdinand fall in love.

As a gift to celebrate their engagement, Prospero calls up the spirits over which he has control to put on a masque. (A *masque* is a small drama with dialogue and song. Originally it meant a play where people donned masks. It is the source of the word, *masquerade*.) While the play is going on, Prospero remembers the threats of Caliban, a rebellious servant who wants to take over the island. Prospero abruptly ends the masque with this speech as the sprits fade away.

In this speech Prospero compares the short masque ("this insubstantial pageant") with the world (the word "globe" here has a double meaning: that is, both our world: the globe, and the London theatre: "The Globe," within which the play *The Tempest* is being performed). Prospero says that just like this pageant ("our revels are ended") the world will eventually come to an end; it will dissolve and leave nothing behind. He also compares our lives to dreams: we come from a sleep and go to a sleep.

Shakespeare often compares life to playing a part on a stage. See "All the world's a stage,…" in *As You Like It* , Act 2; Scene 7; and "Life's …a poor player that struts and frets his hour on the stage…." in *Macbeth* Act 5; Scene 5.

****

Later, in Act 5; Scene 1 of *The Tempest*, Miranda, who has never seen a man before except her father, meets the rest of the shipwrecked comrades of Ferdinand and says,

"O brave new world, that has such people in it."

"Our revels now are ended."

"We are such stuff
 As dreams are made on,...."

from *The Tempest*
Act 4; Scene 1

PROSPERO:

Our revels now are ended. These our actors,
As I foretold you, were all spirits and
Are melted into air, into thin air:
And, like the baseless fabric of this vision,
The cloud-capp'd towers, the gorgeous palaces,
The solemn temples, the great globe itself,
Yea, all which it inherit, shall dissolve
And, like this insubstantial pageant faded,
Leave not a rack behind. We are such stuff
As dreams are made on, and our little life
Is rounded with a sleep.

William Shakespeare

The Sonnet

The **sonnet** is a fourteen-line poem with a very definite organization and rhyme scheme. The greatest poets often wrote sonnets.

The earliest sonnet form was Italian or **Petrarchan,** named after the Italian poet Francisco Petrarca (1304~1374). This kind of sonnet is divided into two parts, the *octave* (the first eight lines) that present a problem or a situation, and the *sestet* (the last six lines) that give the solution to the problem or comment on the situation.

The rhyme scheme of the octave is **a-b-b-a-a-b-b-a**. The rhyme scheme of the sestet might be **c-d-e-c-d-e**, or **c-d-c-d-c-d**, or another variation.

In the sixteenth century (1500~1600) the English developed a form of sonnet that was used by Shakespeare and others and came to be known as the **Shakespearean** sonnet. This kind of poem is written in three *quartets* (four lines in a quartet) and concludes with a couplet (two lines). Like the Petrarchan sonnet, it is divided by sense into an initial, eight-line problem (the first two quartets) and a six-line solution (the third quartet and concluding couplet). The rhyme scheme for the first three quartets is **a-b-a-b, c-d-c-d, e-f-e-f**; with the final couplet rhyme being **g-g**.

Sometimes, as in his "Sonnet 73," (not included in this collection) the three quartets of the Shakespearean sonnet will give three examples of some situation or problem, and the sonnet will conclude with a "rhyming couplet" (two lines) that comments on the previous examples. Again, the rhyme scheme of the first three quartets is **a-b-a-b, c-d-c-d, e-f-e-f**; the final couplet rhyme is **g-g**.

Lines: Sonnets have ten syllables in each line.

Almost every line of a sonnet is written in iambic pentameter. An "iamb" is a 'foot' or 'meter' of rhythm, consisting of a short syllable followed by a long syllable, such as *da dum*. And pentameter (penta=five, meter=feet) means that each line is made up of five of these iambic feet. So each line will sound *da-dum, da-dum, da-dum, da-dum, da-dum*; the natural rhythm of the English language, or as it is frequently called: "the heartbeat."

Sometimes, in order to avoid monotony in a poem, the poet will insert a "foot" that is not iambic, such as a trochee (*long short* as in <u>flower</u>) or a dactyl (*long short short* as in <u>pottery</u>) or an anapaest (*short short long* as four anapaest feet in the poem [not a sonnet] "*He was dressed all in fur / From his head to his foot* "). But no matter the kind of feet or meter, each line in any sonnet will always have ten syllables.

While the three sonnets immediately following this explanation of the sonnet are Shakespearean sonnets, also in this collection are several good examples of Italian or Petrarchan sonnets that can be found on pages 69, 109, 111, 145, 227, and 231, written by John Milton, William Wordsworth, Elizabeth Barret Browning, Gerard Manley Hopkins, and Emma Lazarus respectively.

Notes for **"Sonnet 18"**

Shakespeare's 18th sonnet is one of his most famous, perhaps because of its simplicity. In the octet (the first two quatrains) the poet raises the question of whether he should compare his beloved to a summer's day and then, mostly because of the essential transience of nature, he sets out several reasons why comparison to a summer's day would be inappropriate. In the sestet (the last six lines - a quartet and a couplet) the poet gives the positive reason for withholding such a comparison, namely, that the beloved is not just a summer's day, but an "eternal summer" because the beloved will live on through the poet's writing. As he thinks so highly of the permanence of his verse ("So long as men can breathe or eyes can see, / So long lives this,"), we can assert that there is a bit of a conceit here on the poet's part.

The iambic pentameter rhythm and alternating rhyme scheme with the rhymed couplet at the end both allows the measured words to flow and punctuates the poet's eternal praise for his beloved at the end (see the explanation of **The Sonnet** in this collection).

Interesting here also is the personification in line 11 of "Death" as being unable to "brag" that the beloved walks with the shadow ("shade") of Death always in the future (possibly referring to the 23rd Psalm?), a metaphor echoed in John Donne's sonnet "Death Be Not Proud" that challenges death. Donne's sonnet was published in 1609, coincidentally the same year that Shakespeare's sonnets, though mostly written and circulated in the late 1590s, were published.

"Shall I compare thee to a summer's day?"

SONNET 18

Shall I compare thee to a summer's day?
Thou art more lovely and more temperate:
Rough winds do shake the darling buds of May,
And summer's lease hath all too short a date:
Sometime too hot the eye of heaven shines,*
And often is his gold complexion dimm'd;
And every fair from fair sometime declines,
By chance, or nature's changing course, untrimm'd;
But thy eternal summer shall not fade
Nor lose possession of that fair thou ow'st;*
Nor shall Death brag thou wander'st in his shade,
When in eternal lines to time thou grow'st;*
So long as men can breathe or eyes can see,
So long lives this, and this gives life to thee.

William Shakespeare

* **eye of heaven** = the sun
* **ow'st**   = ownest, i.e. that is yours
* **lines to time**   = blood lines? or lines of verse?
                                      or the wrinkles of age?

Notes for **"Sonnet 29"**

In his 29th sonnet William Shakespeare suggests that there are times when he feels he is in disgrace in the eyes of both fortune (our stars), his associates (men), and when he "alone" beweeps the situation, implying he is keeping this despair to himself, or at least that no one else sympathizes with him.

In the second quatrain (next four lines) he says that in those times of despair he wishes that he had the future prospects, good looks, friends, talent ('art"), and wisdom ('scope") of others whom he sees more fortunate in various ways.

In the eighth line he sums all up saying that even the things he most enjoys, provide him with the least contentment.

Then in the sonnet's sestet, the final six lines (a quartet and Shakespeare's traditional final couplet), his mood changes as he reflects that one person loves him and that brings him happiness. The simile in lines 11 and 12 with the lark (a usual symbol of joy) rising and singing changes the entire mood of the poem from despondency to happiness. The poet moves from lamenting his situation to asserting he would not change his state with kings.

This is a typical Shakespearean sonnet made up of three quartets and a final couplet; the poem is divided by sense into an octet, which sets out the problem, and a sestet that provides a solution. The meter is iambic pentameter, but line one starts with an accented syllable, a device often used by actors in the theatre to get attention. Interestingly, the whole sonnet is composed of one sentence, a semicolon dividing the two major parts.

Shakespeare uses that word "state" three times, the first two referring to his emotional condition, but the last referring possibly to his life as a "kingdom."

"…then I scorn to change my state with kings."

SONNET 29

When, in disgrace with fortune and men's eyes,
I all alone beweep my outcast state,
And trouble deaf heaven with my bootless cries*
And look upon myself, and curse my fate,
Wishing me like to one more rich in hope,
Featur'd like him, like him with friends possess'd*
Desiring this man's art and that man's scope,
With what I most enjoy contented least;
Yet in these thoughts myself almost despising,
Haply I think on thee, and then my state,
Like to the lark at break of day arising
From sullen earth, sings hymns at heaven's gate;
For thy sweet love remember'd such wealth brings
That then I scorn to change my state with kings.

William Shakespeare

* **bootless** = without reward, cf. booty
* **Featur'd** = handsome

Notes for **"Sonnet 116"**

Sonnet 116 is one of Shakespeare's most popular sonnets. Read often at marriages, the first four lines suggest love does not change with "alteration" that is, love does not change if the person loved changes, nor does it change even if the person loved moves away. The second four lines mention that Love is "an ever fixed mark." Here the poet is referring to a lighthouse that is steady, that looks on but is not shaken by storms. Then the poet continues that love, like the lighthouse, is a "star to every wandering bark" (ship), holding the lover steady and keeping him or her from wandering off course. The poet continues with the metaphor suggesting that we can tell the height of a star (that way sailors measure their position on the sea), but we cannot tell much about its worth.

In the last six lines the poet states that love does not change when physical beauty fades, and perhaps that is part of the poet's notion of "alteration" and "remove" in the third and fourth lines. He then suggests that love continues until death. In the last two lines (the closing couplet where Shakespeare generally summarizes his sonnets), the poet writes that if he is in error about love persisting through alterations, removals and impediments, then no man has ever loved.

This poem is often seen as a thesis with the opening line as the topic sentence. Harvard University professor, Helen Vendler, says that if the reader considers the rhythm of the first line "Let ME," (iambic, stressing the "me") the reader might conclude that the poem is a refutation to someone who has just told the poet that various impediments can change love.

William Shakespeare (1564~1616) is considered the greatest playwright and writer in the English language. In addition to thirty-seven plays he also wrote many poems, including a series of 154 sonnets. This sonnet is one of the most famous of the series.

**"Let me not to the marriage of true minds
Admit impediments."**

"It is the star to every wandering bark,...."

SONNET 116

Let me not to the marriage of true minds
Admit impediments. Love is not love
Which alters when it alteration finds,
Or bends with the remover to remove:
O no! it is an ever-fixed mark
That looks on tempests and is never shaken;
It is the star to every wandering bark,
Whose worth's unknown, although his height be taken.
Love's not Time's fool, though rosy lips and cheeks
Within his bending sickle's compass come:
Love alters not with his brief hours and weeks,
But bears it out even to the edge of doom.
If this be error and upon me proved,
I never writ, nor no man ever loved.

William Shakespeare

Notes for John Donne's **"Meditation XVII"**

Although often set to music and sung in many churches, strictly speaking, "No Man is an Island" is not verse or a poem; rather, it is prose. John Donne called it a Meditation. The mid-twentieth century critic, Clifton Fadiman, called it "the greatest sentence in English." The most quoted phrases are "No Man is and Island" and "For Whom the Bell Tolls."

In Donne's time bells were a very important means of public communication. Bells called people to church services and indicated times to pray. At the end of each day the curfew (*couvre* + *feu* = *cover fire*) bell tolled as a signal that all blacksmiths', candle-makers', tanners', and other work fires were to be extinguished. In addition, bells announced funerals. Thus, as soon as the funeral bell started tolling, persons would question each other about who had died, "For whom does the bell toll?"

When the Nobel Prize-winning writer, Ernest Hemingway, wrote his 1940 novel about the Spanish Civil War that took place in the late 1930s, he wanted the book to be a plea for brotherhood and so he titled his novel, *For Whom the Bell Tolls*, knowing intelligent readers would see the reference to Donne's Meditation.

Is Donne right that "Any man's death diminishes me"?

John Donne (1572~1631) was a Roman Catholic poet who in 1614 converted to Anglicanism. He was later ordained a priest and became the dean of St. Paul's Cathedral in London. Along with Shakespeare, Edmund Spencer, Sir Walter Raleigh, Christopher Marlowe, Francis Bacon and Ben Jonson, Donne was one of the many great writers who lived during the time of Queen Elizabeth I, who reigned from 1558 to 1603.

"No man is an island,…."

"…for whom the Bell tolls;…."

from **Devotions on Emergent Occasions**

Meditation XVII

No man is an island, entire of itself;
Every man is a piece of the continent,
A part of the main;   *(main = mainland)*

If a clod be washed away by the sea,
Europe is the less,
As well as if a promontory were,
As well as if a manor of thy friend's or of thine
own were;

Any man's death diminishes me,
because I am involved in mankind,
And therefore never send to know for whom
the bell tolls; it tolls for thee.

John Donne

Notes for **"To the Virgins to Make Much of Time"**

This poem, "To the Virgins to Make Much of Time," published in 1648, reflects a *carpe diem* (Latin for *seize the day*) view of life. Although the first stanzas seem to council a person to do anything she wants, the last stanza specifically urges the reader to marry.

Many poems written in this era have the same theme, possibly because the life span in those days was short. A person was considered old when he or she was fifty, although the author himself lived to be eighty-three. This short poem, which follows a basic **abab** rhyme scheme, was set to music and was a popular song of the 1600s.

Robert Herrick (1591~1674) was an English poet known for his love poems and his poems about the countryside. His poems generally deal with age, the inevitability of death, and suggest the reader take advantage of life's fleeting beauty.

"Gather ye rosebuds while ye may,...."

To the Virgins to Make Much of Time

Gather ye rosebuds while ye may,
  Old Time is still a-flying;
And this same flower that smiles today
  Tomorrow will be dying.

The glorious lamp of heaven, the sun,
  The higher he's a-getting,
The sooner will his race be run,
  And nearer he's to setting.

That age is best which is the first,
  When youth and blood are warmer;
But being spent, the worse, and worst
  Times still succeed the former.

Then be not coy, but use your time,
  And while ye may, go marry;
For having lost but once your prime,
  You may forever tarry.

Robert Herrick

Notes for **"23rd Psalm"**

This psalm is probably the most famous passage in the Bible.

A psalm is a sacred song or hymn, conveying confidence in God, and mostly sung during religious worship services. This particular psalm is worth memorizing in full.

This Psalm is attributed to King David. Although he was a king, David uses the analogy of the shepherd and his flock to say that he, even through evil and difficult times, will be guided by the Lord.

This 23rd Psalm version is from the English translation of the Christian Bible for the Church of England and is known as the *King James Version* of the Bible. By order of King James I, the translation was begun in 1604 by forty-seven scholars, all of whom were Church of England members. Completed and published in 1611, the *King James Version* of the Bible's "New Testament" was translated from Greek, and the "Old Testament" was translated from the Hebrew. The *King James Version* of the Bible is generally considered the most beautiful of all Bible translations.

During the reigns of both King James I and his predecessor Queen Elizabeth I, the modern English language was being formed. Though not participating in the translations of the Bible, the writers living at or about that time were the poets Edmund Spenser and John Donne, playwrights Christopher Marlowe, William Shakespeare and Ben Johnson, as well as writers such as Francis Bacon and Sir Walter Raleigh.

"The Lord is my shepherd;…"

"Though I walk through the valley of the shadow of death, I will fear no evil."

23rd Psalm
King James Bible

The Lord is my shepherd;
I shall not want.
He maketh me to lie down in green pastures;
He leadeth me beside the still waters.
He restoreth my soul;
He leadeth me in the paths of righteousness
For His name's sake.

Yea, though I walk through the valley of
the shadow of death,
I will fear no evil;
for Thou art with me;
Thy rod and thy staff, they comfort me.

Thou preparest a table before me
in the presence of mine enemies;
Thou anointest my head with oil;
My cup runneth over.

Surely goodness and mercy shall follow me
all the days of my life;
And I will dwell in the house of the Lord forever.

Notes for **"Ecclesiastes 3:1-8"**

These eight lines from the third chapter of the Bible's *Book of Ecclesiastes* ask the reader to consider just how to understand, comprehend, and harmonize the apparent duality of this world.

The answer is in the opening line: "To everything there is a season,...," or as commonly stated 'a time and a place for everything,' – "TPO" = a **t**ime, **p**lace and **o**ccasion for everything.

In 1962, with the Vietnam War raging in the early 1960s and resistance the United States' involvement in the war also taking hold around the world, folk singer Pete Seeger used almost the exact words of this biblical passage in a song, "Turn, Turn, Turn," adding a closing line, "I swear it's not too late."

The song, stressing Pete Seeger's additional final line, has often been performed as a plea for world peace. The Byrds performed it and made it more popular in 1965, and Nina Simone performed it in 1968. All these performances are available on YouTube.

"To everything there is a season"

Ecclesiastes 3:1-8
King James Bible

To everything there is a season,
and a time to every purpose under the heaven:

A time to be born, a time to die;
a time to plant,
and a time to pluck up that which is planted;

A time to kill, and a time to heal;
a time to break down, and a time to build up;

A time to weep, and a time to laugh;
a time to mourn, and a time to dance;

A time to cast away stones,
and a time to gather stones together;
a time to embrace,
and a time to refrain from embracing;

A time to get, and a time to lose;
a time to keep, and a time to cast away;

A time to rend, and a time to sew;
a time to keep silence, and a time to speak;

A time to love, and a time to hate;
a time of war, and a time of peace.

Notes for **"First Epistle to the Corinthians"**

Often read at weddings where the word "charity" is translated as "love," this is one of the most famous passages from the "New Testament" of the Bible. The reader might consider whether that difference in translation makes a difference in the meaning of the passage.

In addition, the reader might read William Earnest Henley's "Invictus" and Rudyard Kipling's "If–" in this collection to see how this biblical passage compares, contrasts, and resonates with later verse meanings and forms.

The section here is known as an "epistle," which means a "letter." This version of the "First Epistle of Paul to the Corinthians" is from the English translation of the Christian Bible for the Church of England and is known as the *King James Version* of the Bible. King James I ordered forty-seven scholars to begin the translation in 1604, and the *King James Version* of the Bible was eventually published in 1611.

"…but the greatest of these is charity."

First Epistle to the Corinthians; Chapter 13
King James Bible

Though I speak with the tongues of men, and of angels, and have not charity, I am become as sounding brass, or a tinkling cymbal.

And though I have the gift prophecy, and understanding all mysteries, and all knowledge; and though I have all faith, so that I could remove mountains, and have not charity, I am nothing.

And though I bestow all my goods to feed the poor, and if I should deliver my body to be burned, and have not charity, it profits me nothing.

Charity suffereth long, and is kind: charity envieth not, charity vaunteth not itself; is not puffed up; is not ambitious, seeks not her own, is not provoked to anger, thinks no evil;

Rejoiceth not in iniquity, but rejoiceth in the truth;

Beareth all things, believeth all things, hopeth all things, endureth all things.

Charity never faileth: but whether there be prophecies they shall fail, whether there be tongues, they shall cease, whether there be knowledge, it shall vanish away.

Notes for **"First Epistle to the Corinthians"** (cont.)

The writer of this epistle, Paul, now conventionally known in Christian circles as Saint Paul, was a man living in the first half of the first century of what we now call the "Common Era" or "**CE**," previously known as "AD" from the Latin "anno Domini" meaning 'in the year of our Lord.' "**BCE**" (**B**efore the **C**ommon **E**ra) was previously referred to as "BC" or 'before Christ.' These new and nonreligious designations: **BCE** and **CE** are now the preferred way of referencing history and historical dates before and after the life of Jesus Christ.

Paul was of Jewish ancestry but was a Roman citizen. He was born in Tarsus at a date unknown and appears to have died during the reign of the emperor Nero sometime after 60 CE and before 68 CE. Paul originally persecuted Christians but reversed his beliefs on a trip to the city of Damascus, subsequently becoming a follower of Jesus Christ. Thereafter, Paul travelled around the Mediterranean Sea trying to spread Christ's teachings. Most scholars believe, more than any other single individual, Saint Paul was responsible both for spread of Jesus Christ's teachings and for the swift and broad, overall spread of Christianity.

After a visit to a city during his travels, Paul would write letters (epistles) to the people of that city. Paul's letters were collected as part of the Bible's *New Testament*, and this letter to the people of Corinth may have been written sometime after 51 CE. At that time Corinth (a city at the southern end of a four-mile wide isthmus linking northern and southern Greece) was the Roman Empire's fourth most important city after Rome, Alexandria and Ephesus.

For we know in part, and we prophesy in part.

But when that which is perfect is come, then that which is in part shall be done away.

When I was a child, I spake as a child, I understood as a child, I thought as a child. But, when I became a man, I put away childish things.

For now we see now through a glass darkly; but then face to face; now I know in part; but then I shall know even as also I am known.

And now abideth faith, hope, charity, these three: but the greatest of these is charity.

Saint Paul

Notes for **"Sonnet 19:…"**

This poem is a sonnet in the Italian or Petrarchian style as described on page forty-eight. That is, this is a fourteen-line poem, mostly in iambic pentameter, with the last six lines (actually beginning with "But Patience to prevent…." in line eight) providing an answer to the problem raised in the first eight lines.

Late in his life Milton became blind, and this poem is a meditation on that limitation. Milton expresses his frustration at not being able to serve God as much as he desires, but Patience tells him that God has many others to do his work. God asks only that Milton accept his blindness because persons "…who best bear his mild yoke (an impairment), they serve him best." Milton, realizing that each person serves God in his own way according to his ability, concludes with the famous line, "They also serve who only stand and wait." That is a line worth memorizing.

In what sense is that true for Milton? If he is writing poetry, is he standing and waiting? Is this false modesty?

John Milton, along with Shakespeare and Chaucer, is considered one of the three greatest poets in the English language. His masterpiece is *Paradise Lost,* a long poem, which tells the story of Satan's rebellion against God, his banishment into Hell, and his return to tempt Adam and Eve — causing their fall from the Garden of Eden. Milton says that he wrote *Paradise Lost* to "…assert Eternal Providence, / And justify the ways of God to men." Among Milton's other great poems were *Paradise Regained, Samson Agonistes, L'Allegro* and *Il'Penseroso.* Milton was also a great campaigner for freedom of speech.

"They also serve who only stand and wait."

Sonnet 19:
When I consider how my light is spent

(On his blindness)

When I consider how my light is spent,
Ere half my days, in this dark world and wide,
And that one Talent which is death to hide,
Lodged with me useless, though my Soul more bent
To serve therewith my Maker, and present
My true account, lest he returning chide;
"Doth God exact day-labour, light denied?"
I fondly ask. But patience to prevent
That murmur, soon replies, "God doth not need
Either man's work or his own gifts; who best
Bear his mild yoke, they serve him best, his state
Is Kingly. Thousands at his bidding speed
And post o'er Land and Ocean without rest:
They also serve who only stand and wait."

John Milton

Notes for **"To Lucasta, Going to the Wars"**

* **nunnery** = peacefulness
* **breast** = heart or "being near to you"
* **inconstancy** = not appearing to be constant in my love
  for you

Tough call on this decision, no? Would you leave your sweetheart nowadays to go fight in a war? But that was the code of chivalry back in those days: folks aspiring to the "greater good" of the country (King) rather than their own individual desires. Choosing first to 'embrace' his sword, horse and shield in duty on the battlefield may seem odd, yet the poet here also refers to the importance of chivalrous character, suggesting Lucasta will love him much more if he is a person of honor than if he avoided fighting for his King.

Still, we have both the end-of-the-line rhyming and simple, bigger-than-'self,' thematic overture which propel the reader through this poem. Additionally, the reader might want to also consider the metaphor of, or comparison between, his beloved and war, noting both the words "arms" into which the gentleman 'flies' and the "new mistress" he now "chases."

Richard Lovelace (1618~1657) was an English poet in the seventeenth century. He was a cavalier poet (Cavaliers were those who during the English Civil War [1642-1651] fought on behalf of the King Charles I and against the Roundheads, who supported Parliament's rebellion against the King). His best known works are "To Althea, from Prison," and "To Lucasta, Going to the Wars."

**"I could not love thee (Dear) so much,
Lov'd I not Honour more."**

To Lucasta, Going to the Wars

Tell me not (Sweet) I am unkind,
    That from the nunnery*
Of thy chaste breast and quiet mind*
    To war and arms I fly.

True, a new mistress now I chase,
    The first foe in the field;
And with a stronger faith embrace
    A sword, a horse, a shield.

Yet this inconstancy is such*
    As you too shall adore;
I could not love thee (Dear) so much,
    Lov'd I not Honour more.

Richard Lovelace

Notes for **"To Althea, from Prison"**

* **committed linnets** = caged birds
(linnet = a small finch)
* **hermitage** = a place of quiet for contemplation

The poet writes that even though he is in prison (like a 'committed linnet'), because his mind is free, he is freer than the birds, the fish, and the wind.

In stanza one, the poet says that when his girlfriend visits to show her love, he is as free as the birds.

In stanza two, when, with his friends (*our careless heads*) — and a cup of wine undiluted by water (*Thames*), he can wear a coronet, and with loyal heart, toast (*healths*) and drink (*draughts*) to the King, he is as free as fish in the sea.

In stanza three, when like a caged, singing bird he can sing the praises of his king, he is as free as the wind.

In stanza four, when he has an innocent mind, he is as free as angels

A similar feeling is in the traditional German lyric, "Die Gedanken sind frei" ('The thoughts are free'), and the poet hints that true freedom comes to those who can re-imagine any unpleasant situation be it one of confinement or a place of restriction.

With regard to the image of being like a 'caged bird,' the reader might also reference Paul Laurence Dunbar's "Sympathy" in this collection.

Richard Lovelace (1618~1657) was a seventeenth century English poet. He was also a cavalier poet (Cavaliers were those who during the English Civil War [1642~1651] fought on behalf of the King Charles I and against the Roundheads, who in turn supported the rebellion of Parliament against King Charles I). Lovelace was imprisoned twice by Parliament, and eventually King Charles I was beheaded in 1649. His best known works are "To Althea, from Prison" and "To Lucasta, Going to the Wars."

"Stone walls do not a Prison make, Nor iron bars a Cage;...."

To Althea, from Prison

When Love with unconfinéd wings
Hovers within my Gates,
And my divine *Althea* brings
To whisper at the Grates;
When I lie tangled in her hair
And fettered to her eye,
The birds that wanton in the Air
Know no such Liberty.

When flowing Cups run swiftly round,
With no allaying *Thames*,
Our careless heads with roses bound,
Our hearts with Loyal Flames;
When thirsty grief in Wine we steep,
When Healths and draughts go free,
Fishes, that tipple in the Deep,
Know no such Liberty.

When, like committed linnets, I*
With shriller throat shall sing
The sweetness, Mercy, Majesty,
And glories of my King;
When I shall voice aloud how good
He is, how great should be,
Enlargéd winds, that curl the Flood,
Know no such Liberty.

Stone walls do not a Prison make,
Nor iron bars a Cage;
Minds innocent and quiet take
That for a Hermitage.*
If I have freedom in my Love,
And in my soul am free,
Angels alone, that soar above,
Enjoy such Liberty.

Richard Lovelace

Notes for **"To His Coy Mistress"**

***** = lines omitted

* **Humber** = a river in England with high tides

This poem is Andrew Marvell's most famous and reflects the "carpe diem" (Latin for *seize the day*) view of many persons of that time, possibly because of their short life spans. Note how marvelously Marvell's first stanza sets up the tension and standoff between the man's complaining advances ("ten years before the flood") and the woman's forever refusals or push-backs against those advances ("Till the conversion of the Jews" — which, of course, will never happen). Yet, by the second-to-last stanza, the gentleman's overtures now bring on the seductive warning of time's own marching advance; death within a constant earshot. Finally, the last stanza pitches an unrestrained acceleration of desire: since we're not going to stop the advance of time, let's advance *our* own cause, our own "sport," and "Our sweetness into one ball,..." and "tear our pleasures with rough strife / Through the iron gates of life:...."

"Had we but world enough and time" is a much-quoted line, and the phrase "World Enough and Time" has been used for both book and movie titles.

Andrew Marvell (1621~1678) was an English lyric poet who became an assistant to John Milton when Milton was a secretary in the Commonwealth government of Oliver Cromwell (1653~1658). Marvell was also a friend of Richard Lovelace, although Lovelace was both a Royalist and supporter of King Charles I, who was beheaded in 1649. After the restoration of the monarchy, whereby Charles II became King of England in 1660, Marvell defended Milton and managed to keep Milton out of prison.

"Had we but world enough and time,…"
To His Coy Mistress

Had we but world enough and time,
This coyness, lady, were no crime.
We would sit down, and think which way
To walk, and pass our long love's day.
Thou by the Indian Ganges' side
Shouldst rubies find; I by the tide
Of Humber would complain. I would*
Love you ten years before the flood,
And you should, if you please, refuse
Till the conversion of the Jews.
*****

But at my back I always hear
Time's wingèd chariot hurrying near;
And yonder all before us lie
Deserts of vast eternity.
Thy beauty shall no more be found;
Nor, in thy marble vault, shall sound
My echoing song; then worms shall try
That long-preserved virginity,
And your quaint honour turn to dust,
And into ashes all my lust;
The grave's a fine and private place,
But none, I think, do there embrace.

Now therefore, while the youthful hue
Sits on thy skin like morning dew,
And while thy willing soul transpires
At every pore with instant fires,
Now let us sport us while we may,
And now, like amorous birds of prey,
Rather at once our time devour
Than languish in his slow-chapped power.
Let us roll all our strength and all
Our sweetness up into one ball,
And tear our pleasures with rough strife
Through the iron gates of life:
Thus, though we cannot make our sun
Stand still, yet we will make him run.

Andrew Marvell

Notes for **"Happy the Man"**

It might be said that Dryden was more "inspired" by Horace than precisely translating his ode. Here are Horace's original Latin words, each line followed by a modern English translation of his lines in italics.

ille potens sui / laetusque deget, cui licet in diem
He is happy / content who can each day

dixisse "vixi: cras vel atra
say, 'I have lived: tomorrow

nube polum Pater occupato
Father (Jupiter) who occupies the mountains topped with clouds

vel sole puro; non tamen irritum,
Or in the bright sun; will not

quodcumque retro est, efficiet neque
alter whatever has been done, nor

diffinget infectumque reddet,
take back and undo

quod fugiens semel hora vexit."
what once the hour that has passed has changed.'

Horace (65 BCE~8 BCE) was the most famous Roman poet in the time of Augustus Caesar. He was in the army of Brutus and Cassius that was defeated at the Battle of Philippi in 42 BCE by Mark Antony and Augustus Caesar's army. He was offered and accepted amnesty. Horace was best known for his odes; Alexander Pope praised him saying "What oft was thought, but ne'er so well expressed;...." (p. 81; line 300 in this collection). Horace published this ode (a short poem) with a number of others in 23 BCE.

John Dryden (1631~1700) was an English poet, dramatist and translator. He and John Milton were the most famous poets of the middle 1600s. Dryden was the first Poet Laureate of England and also became the leading literary critic of his time. He is also credited with standardizing the "heroic couplet" (a pair of rhymed lines in iambic pentameter) as a literary convention in satires, plays, fables, epigrams, religious pieces and prologues.

"Happy the man…."

"Tomorrow do thy worst, for I have lived today."

"…I have had my hour"

Happy the Man

Happy the man, and happy he alone,
He who can call today his own:
He who, secure within, can say,
Tomorrow do thy worst, for I have lived today.
Be fair or foul or rain or shine
The joys I have possessed, in spite of fate, are mine.
Not Heaven itself upon the past has power,
But what has been, has been,
And I have had my hour.

from **Horace's** Ode
Book III; Ode 29, lines 41-48
Translation by *John Dryden*

Notes for **"Essay on Criticism"**

Part I

Alexander Pope's *Essay on Criticism*, written when he was twenty-one, attempts to show and demonstrate how to be a good critic. The poem is written in "heroic couplets," that is, two iambic pentameter lines that rhyme, a form of verse in which Pope was an expert. It seemed to come naturally to him. The most important writer of the mid-eighteenth century Dr. Samuel Johnson said the *Essay on Criticism* "...displays such extent of comprehension, such nicety of distinction, such acquaintance with mankind, and such knowledge of both ancient and modern learning as are not often attained by those of maturest age and longest experience."

As noted, these quoted lines are only excerpts from a 744-line poem. They demonstrate not only Alexander Pope's ability to create a memorable phrase but also the poet's ability to offer practical advice. Other poets' practical advice in this collection can be found both in Rudyard Kipling's "If—" and Edward Fitzgerald's "The Rubaiyat of Omar Khayyam."

The *Essay on Criticism* falls into three parts. In Part I (lines 1-202) the poet suggests that poor judging is worse than poor writing because poor writing only bores the reader, but poor judging misleads the reader. He says that a critic should both know the limits of his power and should study classic writers.

"A little Learning is a dang'rous thing;...."

"...To err is human, to forgive, divine."

"...For Fools rush in where Angels fear to tread."

An Essay on Criticism
(excerpts)

***** = lines omitted

from **Part I**

1 'Tis hard to say, if greater want of skill
2 Appear in writing or in judging ill;
3 But, of the two, less dang'rous is th' offence
4 To tire our patience, than mislead our sense.
*****

9 'Tis with our judgments as our watches, none
10 Go just alike, yet each believes his own.
11 In Poets as true Genius is but rare,
12 True Taste as seldom is the Critic's share;
13 Both must alike from heav'n derive their light,
14 These born to judge, as well as those to write.
*****

46 But you who seek to give and merit fame,
47 And justly bear a Critic's noble name,
48 Be sure yourself and your own reach to know,
49 How far your genius, taste, and learning go;
50 Launch not beyond your depth, but be discreet,
51 And mark that point where sense and dullness meet.
*****

139 Learn hence for ancient rules a just esteem;
140 To copy nature is to copy them.
*****

Notes for **"Essay on Criticism"** (cont.)

**Line 218, "Pierian Spring," refers to a particular spring sacred to the Muses in the Pierian Mountains of Macedonia.

In Part II (lines 203-561) Pope suggests that good judgment can be hindered by pride, by imperfect learning, by prejudice, and by envy as well as by not appreciating language or by judging the parts but not the whole.

In the often quoted lines 364 to 375 Pope demonstrates how the sound of a line should echo its sense.

from **Part II**

203 Of all the causes which conspire to blind
204 Man's erring judgment, and misguide the mind,
205 What the weak head with strongest bias rules,
206 Is Pride, the never-failing vice of fools.
*****

217 A little Learning is a dang'rous thing;
218 Drink deep, or taste not the Piërian spring: **
219 There shallow draughts intoxicate the brain,
220 And drinking largely sobers us again.
*****

299 True wit is nature to advantage dress'd,
300 What oft' was thought, but ne'er so well express'd;
*****

311 Words are like leaves; and where they most
abound,
312 Much fruit of sense beneath is rarely found.
*****

337 Be not the first by whom the new are try'd,
338 Nor yet the last to lay the old aside.
*****

364 True ease in writing comes from art, not chance,
365 As those move easiest who have learn'd to dance.
366 'Tis not enough no harshness gives offence,
367 The sound must seem an echo to the sense.
368 Soft is the strain when Zephyr gently blows,
369 And the smooth stream in smoother numbers flows;
370 But when loud surges lash the sounding shore,
371 The hoarse, rough verse should like the torrent roar.
372 When Ajax strives, some rock's vast weight to throw,
373 The line too labours, and the words move slow;
374 Not so, when swift Camilla scours the plain,
375 Flies o'er th'unbending corn, and skims along the
main.
*****

526 Good-nature and good-sense must ever join;
527 To err is human, to forgive, divine.
*****

Notes for **"Essay on Criticism"** (cont.)

Part III

In Part III (lines 562-end) the poet further suggests that knowing what is good is only half the job; most important are the manners and the character of a good critic: truthfulness, modesty, sincerity and restraint.

Alexander Pope (1688~1744) was an English poet and essayist. He, along with Joseph Addison, Richard Steele, and particularly his great friend Jonathan Swift were considered the chief writers of the early eighteenth century. Although he had privately circulated a number of admired poems called *Pastorals*, Pope's *Essay on Criticism,* published in 1709 when he was twenty-one, was his first major work and it brought him great fame. Pope was frail and small (he is said to have been four foot, six inches tall) with curvature of the spine. He learned the rudiments of Greek and Latin early, and from the age of twelve, he was self-educated. His later works included *The Rape of the Lock*, translations of Virgil and Homer, the *Dunciad*, and the *Essay on Man*.

from **Part III**

562 Learn then what Morals Critics ought to show,
563 For 'tis but half a judge's task, to know.
564 'Tis not enough, wit, art, and learning join;
565 In all you speak, let truth and candour shine:
566 That not alone what to your judgment's due
567 All may allow; but seek your friendship too.
568 Be silent always when you doubt your sense;
569 And speak, tho' sure, with seeming diffidence:
*****

574 'Tis not enough, your counsel still be true;
575 Blunt truths more mischief than nice falsehoods do;
576 Men must be taught as if you taught them not,
577 And things unknown propos'd as things forgot.
*****

626 Nay, fly to Alters; there they'll talk you dead;
627 For Fools rush in where Angels fear to tread.
*****

Alexander Pope

Notes for
"Elegy Written in a Country Churchyard"

An elegy is a serious reflection, typically a lament (expression of grief and/or sorrow) for the dead.

"Elegy in a Country Churchyard" (a 128-line poem; only thirty-six of which are replicated here), describes an evening (first stanza here) during which the poet visits a graveyard (second stanza here) and then thinks about all the poor people buried there, some who, because of where they were born and because of their condition of poverty, never had a chance for greatness.

Because of the eighteenth century language, the first two lines are hard to understand.

(*first line*)

"The curfew tolls the knell of parting day,..."

* **curfew** = the evening bell (usually from the church steeple), signaling the time for fires to be put out (curfew means 'cover the fire').
* **tolls** = rings (with implication of death, e.g. Donne "For whom the bell tolls")
* **knell** = the sound of a bell announcing death

This first line sets the tone of the poem, that is, **an elegy** (a poem about the dead) and the words "tolls" and "knell" imitate the sound of a bell.

(*second line*)

"The lowing herd wind slowly o'er the lea,...."
= the mooing or bellowing (lowing) cows (herd) move or walk(wind) slowly over the grassy meadow (lea).

* **glebe** = cultivated land
* **jocund** = happily
* **unfathomed** = unmeasured. A fathom is a measure of sea depth.

"The paths of glory lead but to the grave."

Elegy Written in a Country Churchyard
(excerpts) ***** = lines omitted

The curfew tolls the knell of parting day,*
The lowing herd wind slowly o'er the lea,*
The ploughman homeward plods his weary way,
And leaves the world to darkness and to me.
*****

Beneath those rugged elms, that yew-tree's shade,
Where heaves the turf in many a mouldering heap,
Each in his narrow cell for ever laid,
The rude forefathers of the hamlet sleep.
*****

For them no more the blazing hearth shall burn,
Or busy housewife ply her evening care:
No children run to lisp their sire's return,
Or climb his knees the envied kiss to share.

Oft did the harvest to their sickle yield,
Their furrow oft the stubborn glebe has broke;*
How jocund did they drive their team afield!*
How bowed the woods beneath their sturdy stroke!

Let not Ambition mock their useful toil,
Their homely joys, and destiny obscure;
Nor Grandeur hear with a disdainful smile,
The short and simple annals of the poor.

The boast of heraldry, the pomp of power,
And all that beauty, all that wealth e'er gave,
Awaits alike the inevitable hour.
The paths of glory lead but to the grave.

Notes for **"Elegy Written in a Country...."** (cont.)

An often quoted line from this poem is: "The paths of glory lead but to the grave," meaning no matter how powerful, wealthy or beautiful a person is, he or she must inevitably die.

Other famous lines are: "Full many a flower is born to blush unseen, And waste its sweetness on the desert air," meaning that there are many beautiful and talented persons buried here who were never recognized outside their small town.

An **epitaph** is a phrase or statement written in memory of a person who has died, especially as an inscription on a tombstone.

Thomas Gray (1716~1771) was an English poet and letter writer, who is often considered one of the first Romantic poets (preceding Wordsworth, Keats, Shelley, Coleridge). Except for a short time in London, he lived in Cambridge where in 1768 he accepted a Professorship in History. He began writing poetry in 1742 and this poem, published in 1751, made him known to the public. The eminent eighteenth century critic Dr. Samuel Johnson said that the Elegy "abounds with images which find a mirror in every mind, and with sentiments to which every bosom returns an echo."

Full many a gem of purest ray serene,
The dark unfathomed caves of ocean bear:*
Full many a flower is born to blush unseen,
And waste its sweetness on the desert air.
*****

The Epitaph

Here rests his head upon the lap of earth
A youth to fortune and to fame unknown.
Fair Science frowned not on his humble birth,
And Melancholy marked him for her own.

*****

No farther seek his merits to disclose,
Or draw his frailties from their dread abode,
(There they alike in trembling hope repose)
The bosom of his Father and his God.

Thomas Gray

Notes for **"The Solitude of Andrew Selkirk"**

In 1704, Alexander Selkirk, a second mate on an English ship, after a quarrel with the ship's captain, asked to be put off to live on a deserted island near Chile. He remained there until picked up by another English ship in 1709.

In 1713, the essayist Richard Steele wrote about Selkirk's deserted island stay, and Steele's essay about Selkirk's story is considered to have been the inspiration for Daniel DeFoe's *Robinson Crusoe* published in 1719.

This poem is notable for its irony (saying the opposite of what you mean) because its first stanza is repudiated by the rest of the poem.

The opening lines were also used by Henry David Thoreau in *Walden* published in 1854, though not in an ironic sense.

For extended irony in speech, see Mark Antony's speech in Shakespeare's *Julius Caesar,* Act 3, Scene 2 (in this collection).

"I am the monarch of all I survey,...."

The Solitude of Alexander Selkirk

I am monarch of all I survey,
My right there is none to dispute,
From the center all round to the sea,
I am lord of the fowl and the brute.

O Solitude! where are the charms
That sages have seen in thy face?
Better dwell in the midst of alarms
Than reign in this horrible place.

I am out of humanity's reach,
I must finish my journey alone,
Never hear the sweet music of speech, —
I start at the sound of my own.

The beasts that roam over the plain
My form with indifference see;
They are so unacquainted with man,
Their tameness is shocking to me.

Society, Friendship, and Love,
Divinely bestow'd upon man,
Oh, had I the wings of a dove,
How soon would I taste you again!

My sorrows I then might assuage
In the way of religion and truth;
Might learn from the wisdom of age,
And be cheer'd by the sallies of youth.

Notes for **"The Solitude of Andrew Selkirk"** (cont.)

William Cowper (1731~1800) was a very popular English poet and translator who wrote in the era between the classical tradition of Alexander Pope and the Romantic tradition of William Wordsworth. In writing his own version of what Alexander Selkirk's thoughts might have been during Selkirk's self-imposed exile on the island, William Cowper published this poem in 1782.

Ye winds that have made me your sport,
Convey to this desolate shore
Some cordial endearing report
Of a land I shall visit no more:

My friends — do they now and then send
A wish or a thought after me?
Oh, tell me I yet have a friend,
Though a friend I am never to see.

How fleet is a glance of the mind!
Compared with the speed of its flight,
The tempest itself lags behind,
And the swift-winged arrows of light.

When I think of my own native land,
In a moment I seem to be there;
But alas! recollection at hand
Soon hurries me back to despair.

But the seafowl is gone to her nest,
The beast is laid down in his lair,
Even here is a season of rest,
And I to my cabin repair.

There's mercy in every place,
And mercy, encouraging thought!
Gives even affliction a grace,
And reconciles man to his lot.

William Cowper

Notes for **"The Tyger"**

Here Blake compares God's and the blacksmith's creative, framing or shaping powers. Creating with free will, the blacksmith heats metal with fire, hammering and twisting into shape his creations. You can almost hear the hammer blows or whacks in the repeated word "what, what, what" as the blacksmith hammers away. Yet is the blacksmith aware (as God is in creating both Tyger and Lamb) that he can create good and evil from the sometimes "twisted" creations of his free will? Are the angels (stars) throwing spears and weeping at the uncertainty of mankind's creative free will? Come these creations from hell ("distant deeps") or heaven ("skies")?

A blacksmith usually smiles to see his completed work (as we all do when we complete a hard task), and the poet then asks whether or not God too smiled to see not only the tiger and lamb that He created but also man, who is also capable of creating both good and evil from the 'furnace' of his brain.

William Blake (1757~1827) was an English poet, painter and engraver. He was very religious, although not of any particular denomination. His collected works include *Songs of Innocence* and *Songs of Experience* (sometimes coupled in one volume as *Songs of Innocence and Experience*).

Blake loved nature, basic handmade articles and very much lamented the industrial takeover of so much of the English countryside. Blake penned "The Lamb" in 1789, probably his most famous poem in *Songs of Innocence*. "The Tyger" came five years later in 1794 in *Songs of Experience*, perhaps reflecting Blake's disdain for industrialization.

Blake, perhaps the Romantic writer who exerted the greatest influence on the twentieth century, also had incredible influence on both the 1950s Beat poets, such as Allen Ginsberg, and 1960s counterculture songwriters, such as Bob Dylan, Jim Morrison and Van Morrison. Incidentally, the rock band U2's 2014 album is called *Songs of Innocence*, and their next effort is to be called *Songs of Experience*.

"Tyger! Tyger! Burning Bright...."

The Tyger

Tyger! Tyger! burning bright
In the forests of the night,
What immortal hand or eye
Could frame thy fearful symmetry?

In what distant deeps or skies
Burnt the fire of thine eyes?
On what wings dare he aspire?
What the hand dare seize the fire?

And what shoulder & what art.
Could twist the sinews of thy heart?
And when thy heart began to beat,
What dread hand? & what dread feet?

What the hammer? what the chain?
In what furnace was thy brain?
What the anvil? what dread grasp
Dare its deadly terrors clasp?

When the stars threw down their spears,
And watered heaven with their tears,
Did he smile his work to see?
Did he who made the Lamb make thee?

Tyger! Tyger! burning bright
In the forests of the night,
What immortal hand or eye
Dare frame thy fearful symmetry?

William Blake

Notes for *Auguries of Innocence* (opening lines)

This is a poem of creation, beauty, space, time, and the interrelationship of all in the universe. The atoms in a grain of sand are similar to the atoms in every material thing, and so the grain of sand is neither different from the world nor the universe.

Seeing heaven in a wild flower, the poet here is encouraging the reader to perceive eternal and infinite beauty in color and shape through our senses of sight, smell, and touch. Even within that beauty is also the utility of relationship between all and mankind; beneficial as it also can be terrifying and prophetic. Is our idea of heaven an idea of all kinds of beauty, a fearful, earthly beauty as well as unfathomable beauty?

Infinity is not limited. The area in the palm of one's hand is finite; it is of limited space — or so it would seem. Held in the supposed limited space of a human palm, either a 'grain of sand' or the perfect geometry of a flower's stamen, pistils and petals can yield limitless observations: 'a world' if you will. Does Blake ask us to grasp the intimacy of our interrelationship with all things of the world, if not of and with infinity itself?

And what is an hour? Like a minute, a measure of time for most of us; a workday's basic measure. But before hours were invented; that is, before clocks, time could not be measured accurately. Eternity is outside of time, and since it cannot be measured, what can and/or do our senses really "measure"? What do we really "know" through measurement?

Thus, here, time, space, size and beauty intermingle a world of infinite relationships! Is the poet signaling to us that beauty's creation and/or the perception thereof, even from the smallest of elemental building-blocks, is, or can be, in our own hands, right-here-and-now?

William Blake (1757~1857) was an English poet, painter and engraver. He was very religious, although not of any particular denomination. His collected works include *Songs of Innocence* and *Songs of Experience* (sometimes coupled in one volume as *Songs of Innocence and Experience*).

"To see a World in a Grain of Sand...."

opening lines from *Auguries of Innocence*

To see a World in a Grain of Sand
And a Heaven in a Wild Flower
Hold Infinity in the palm of your hand
And Eternity in an hour....

William Blake

Notes for **"Jerusalem"**

In "Jerusalem" the poet obviously does not appreciate the "dark satanic mills," the factories, that he sees in the mountains, pastures, and now "clouded (smoke-filled), hills" of England. What is the Jerusalem the poet says "we" will build? Is it just the green and pleasant land? Who is the "we" that he seems to be addressing?

Why does the poet ask for his sword, arrows and chariot of fire, if the "fight" that he will undertake is "mental"? Are the arrows, spear and chariot the poet's words?

The poem's end-of-the-third-stanza phrase "…Chariot of fire…." was pluralized to become "Chariots of Fire" and then used as the title of a 1981 award winning movie about two British track athletes, one a determined Jew and the other a devout Christian, who competed in the 1924 Olympics.

William Blake (1757~1857) was an English poet, painter and engraver. He was very religious, although not of any particular denomination. His collected works include *Songs of Innocence* and *Songs of Experience* (sometimes coupled in one volume as *Songs of Innocence and Experience*). Blake loved nature, basic handmade articles, and very much lamented the industrialization of so much of England's pastoral countryside.

Two of Blake's most famous poems are "The Tyger" and this fragment called "Jerusalem." These words, having been put to a musical score, have since become a kind of British anthem, and "Jerusalem" was thus sung in London during the opening ceremony of the 2012 Summer Olympics.

"Bring me my Chariot of fire!"

Jerusalem
["And did those feet in ancient time"]

from "Preface to Milton" (1804)

And did those feet in ancient time,
Walk upon Englands mountains green:
And was the holy Lamb of God,
On Englands pleasant pastures seen!

And did the Countenance Divine
Shine forth upon our clouded hills?
And was Jerusalem builded here
Among these dark Satanic Mills?

Bring me my Bow of burning gold;
Bring me my Arrows of desire:
Bring me my Spear! O clouds, unfold!
Bring me my Chariot of fire!

I will not cease from Mental Fight,
Nor shall my sword sleep in my hand:
Till we have built Jerusalem,
In Englands green & pleasant Land.

William Blake

Notes for **"Auld Lang Syne"**

* **auld lang syne** = literally "old long since" or "long time ago"

  my jo = my friend,
* **ye'll be your pint-stowp!** = you'll buy your jug pint
* **We twa hae run about the brae** = we two have run about the hills
* **And pu'd the gowans fine;** = and pulled the daisies fine
* **But** = And
* **paidl'd i' the burn** = paddled in the stream
* **mornin' sun till dine;** = from morning to dinner time
* **braid hae roar'd** = broad have roared
* **my trusty fiere!** = my trusty friend
* **gie's a hand o' thine** = and give us a hand of yours
* **guid willy waught** = a right drink of good will and friendship

The actual origin of this poem of friendship: *Auld Lang Syne* is unknown. Robert Burns wrote to a friend that it was "an old song of olden times which has never been in print … I took it down from an old man's singing." Burns no doubt added verses to the original and so the poem is considered his.

The verses, written about 1788, were not intended to be a holiday song. However, Guy Lombardo, a leader of a very popular orchestra called "The Royal Canadians," used an English version of the song on a live radio broadcast from a night club at the Roosevelt Hotel in New York City just after the clock hit midnight in 1929 to begin the new year of 1930. The live audience in the night club sang along during the chorus and the radio audience loved it. Although there are some earlier documented instances of others singing this song on New Year's Eve, it was Lombardo's 1929 performance that made it the New Year's Eve tradition that now extends throughout the world.

Robert Burns (1759~1796) is considered the national poet of Scotland. He is known for his lyrical poems written in the Scottish vernacular about nature, love, and patriotism.

"Should auld acquaintance be forgot,…."
"… we'll tak a cup o' kindness yet,…."

Auld Lang Syne

Should auld acquaintance be forgot,
And never brought to mind?
Should auld acquaintance be forgot,
And days of auld lang syne.

Chorus:
For auld lang syne, my jo,*
For auld lang syne,
We'll tak a cup o' kindness yet,
For auld lang syne,

And surely ye'll be your pint-stowp!*
And surely I'll be mine!
And we'll tak a cup o' kindness yet,
For auld lang syne.
Chorus

We twa hae run about the brae*
And pu'd the gowans fine;*
But we've wander'd mony a weary foot*
Sin auld lang syne.
Chorus

We twa hae paidl'd i' the burn,*
Frae mornin' sun till dine;*
But seas between us braid hae roar'd*
Sin auld lang syne.
Chorus

And there's a hand, my trusty fiere!*
And gie's a hand o' thine!*
And we'll tak a right guid willy waught,*
For auld lang syne.
Chorus

Robert Burns

Notes for **"To a Mouse"**

The story: the poet's plough crashes through the mouse's burrow, and the mouse flees in panic. The poet has upset the plans of the mouse, who thought it had a cozy home for the winter. The poet ends by suggesting because the mouse lives only in the present, it has an advantage compared to the poet. The poet, because he is a human, can both see his dreary past and worry about his unknown future. The mouse, in contrast, is of the present, free from both the past and future.

The poem contains one of the most quoted lines in the English language:

> **"The best laid schemes o' mice an' men
> gang aft agley."**

(or in modern English)

> **"The best laid plans of mice and men often
> go astray."**

When twentieth century Nobel prize-winning writer John Steinbeck wrote his famous short novel *Of Mice and Men* in 1937, he expected thoughtful readers to realize from the title he chose that the plans of the characters in his short novel might not go as they expected.

"The best laid schemes o' Mice an' Men often go astray."

To a Mouse

On Turning up in Her Nest with the Plough,
November, 1785

***** = omitted stanzas
under *italics* = modern English

Wee, sleeket, cowran, tim'rous beastie,
   Small crafty cowering timerous animal,
O, what a panic's in thy breastie!
   O what a panic is in your breast!
Thou need na start awa sae hasty,
   You need not run away so fast,
Wi' bickerin brattle!
   With broken chatter!
I wad be laith to rin an' chase thee
   I would be reluctant to chase you
Wi' murd'ring pattle!
   With murdering spade!

I'm truly sorry Man's dominion
Has broken Nature's social union,
An' justifies that ill opinion,
  Which makes thee startle,
At me, thy poor, earth-born companion,
  An' fellow-mortal!
*****

Thy wee-bit housie, too, in ruin!
   Your small house too, in ruin!
It's silly wa's the win's are strewin!
   Its feeble walls strewn about by the wind!
An' naething, now, to big a new ane,
   And nothing now to build a new one,

Notes for **"To a Mouse"** (cont.)

Robert Burns (1759~1796) was, perhaps, the most famous of all Scottish poets. This poem reveals how he felt sympathy with all mortal things. Many suggest that Robert Burns continues to be the national poet of Scotland in that much of Scottish literature ends with him before giving way to English poetry or some 'Anglified' versions of Scottish verse. On the other hand, Burns, showing great sensitivity to nature and man's 'turn' within it, championing individualism and freedom against authority, supporting all interests in old songs and folklore, and writing with great emotion and feeling, might be said to have been at the front of the Romantic Movement; a pre-Romantic poet if you will.

Along with his humble, agricultural beginnings, Robert Burns struggled with the changing English language, as rural production moved to urban centers, printing presses started replacing the written word (making the Scottish even more dependent upon London and the British), and the industrial revolution was rapidly displacing traditional culture.

In 1782 Robert Burns also wrote a poem, actually a jingle in two settings, entitled "Comin thro' the Rye," which is thought to be the basis of where the title of J.D. Salinger's famous 1951 novel *The Catcher in the Rye* originated. In Chapter 16 of the story, Holden Caulfield, the protagonist, notices a boy walking in the street (instead of on the sidewalk) 'singing and humming' the phrase: "If a body catch a body coming through the rye." Burns' lyrics are a little different:

> **"Comin thro' the rye, poor body,**
>   **Comin thro' the rye...."**

and later in the second setting of Burns' poem:

> **"Gin a body meet a body, comin thro' the rye...."**

While not sung exactly word for word by the boy in the street, the boy's jingle becomes Holden Caulfield's reason for living, as he tells his sister Phoebe in Chapter 22: "I'd just be the catcher in the rye and all. I know it's crazy, but that's the only thing I'd really like to be." Read Robert Burn's poem and *The Catcher in the Rye* and discover vernacular Scottish phrasing and the connection to Holden's raison d'être in the novel.

O' foggage green!
Of course green grass!
An' bleak December's winds ensuin,
And bleak December's winds are coming,
Baith snell an' keen!
Both sharp and keen!
An' weary Winter comin fast,
An' cozie here, beneath the blast,
And cosy here beneath the blast,
Thou thought to dwell,
Till crash! the cruel coulter past
Till crash, the cruel plough came
Out thro' thy cell.
Through your home.
*****

But Mousie, thou art no thy-lane,
But Mouse, you are not alone,
In proving foresight may be vain:
The best laid schemes o' Mice an' Men
Gang aft agley.
Often go astray.
An' lea'e us nought but grief an' pain,
For promis'd joy!
Still, thou art blest, compar'd wi' me!
The present only toucheth thee:
But Och! I backward cast my e'e,
On prospects drear!
An' forward tho' I canna see,
I guess an' fear!

Robert Burns

Notes for **"I Wandered Lonely as a Cloud"**

* **jocund** = *pleasant, happy, blithe, light hearted*

Embedded in this poem's **ababcc** rhyme scheme, with final, stanza-ending rhymed-couplets throughout, is the meandering author's singular existence, beginning to end: at first lonely then not with "heart with pleasure fills....," taken over in rapture with the dance of golden daffodils.

Moreover, within the poem are a couple of metaphors (*similes* to be exact) as well as comparisons that link the earth and sky; water and land. Can you find them? Additionally, this poem features the poetic device of personification, attributing human characteristics or qualities to animals, objects or ideas. Considering the daffodils, what two human attributes are given to the flowers by Wordsworth?

For a more extensive treatment of *metaphor* and *personification* in this collection, see "The Landlord's Tale. Paul Revere's Ride" on pages 154-161.

Wordsworth both reminds us of both the natural "wealth" through which we wander each and every day – as well as the very treasures – should we see the universal links, we can carry in our mind's eye and hearts for the rest of our lives.

William Wordsworth (1770~1850), being appointed Poet Laureate of England in 1843, was, along with Coleridge, Shelley, and Keats, the leader of the Romantic Movement in poetry. Wordsworth is known for his worship of nature. He tried to write in "the language really used by men." Wordsworth said that poetry was "emotion recalled in tranquility." That is evident in the last stanza of this poem as well as in "The Solitary Reaper." His long and famous poem, "Lines Composed a Few Miles above Tintern Abbey, On Revisiting the Banks of the Wye during a Tour. July 13, 1798" also reflects this view of poetry.

"I wandered lonely as a cloud…."

I Wandered Lonely as a Cloud

I wandered lonely as a cloud
That floats on high o'er vales and hills,
When all at once I saw a crowd,
A host, of golden daffodils;
Beside the lake, beneath the trees,
Fluttering and dancing in the breeze.

Continuous as the stars that shine
And twinkle on the milky way,
They stretched in never-ending line
Along the margin of a bay:
Ten thousand saw I at a glance,
Tossing their heads in sprightly dance.

The waves beside them danced; but they
Out-did the sparkling waves in glee:
A poet could not but be gay,
In such a jocund company:*
I gazed–and gazed–but little thought
What wealth the show to me had brought:

For oft, when on my couch I lie
In vacant or in pensive mood,
They flash upon that inward eye
Which is the bliss of solitude;
And then my heart with pleasure fills,
And dances with the daffodils.

William Wordsworth

Notes for **"The Solitary Reaper"**

* **chaunt** = chant or sing
* **Hebrides** = islands off the west coast of Scotland
* **numbers** = metrics or number of syllables in a line
  and by extension here: "poetry."
* **lay** = a song

Perhaps the most salient, interpretive feature of this poem comes as the song the girl sings, while "...she cuts and binds the grain....," also *cuts and binds* into the author's own heart as he passes on 'up the hill' and carries the maiden's profoundly curious tune onward just as her grain bundles will eventually be carried onward to the mill or market. Thus, in suggesting the working maiden's melancholy song to be even more comforting, fulfilling, and everlasting than the songs of two types of birds, each character here: the 'highland lass' and the poet, will carry away different 'harvests' so to speak: that which sustains us physically and that which sustains us spiritually.

Again, both Wordsworth's mastery of end-line rhyme and words of the common man give his verse a contemporary song of its own. And after all, isn't it nice and comforting now-and-then to "carry a tune," recalling experience and song from memory?

William Wordsworth (1770~1850) was an English poet known for his worship of nature. He tried to write in "the language really used by men." He was appointed poet laureate of England in 1843. Wordsworth said that poetry was "emotion recalled in tranquility." That is evident in the last two lines of this poem.

**"The music in my heart I bore,
  Long after it was heard no more."**

The Solitary Reaper

Behold her, single in the field,
Yon solitary Highland Lass!
Reaping and singing by herself;
Stop here, or gently pass!
Alone she cuts and binds the grain,
And sings a melancholy strain;
O listen! for the Vale profound
Is overflowing with the sound.

No Nightingale did ever chaunt*
More welcome notes to weary bands
Of travellers in some shady haunt,
Among Arabian sands:
A voice so thrilling ne'er was heard
In spring-time from the Cuckoo-bird,
Breaking the silence of the seas
Among the farthest Hebrides.*

Will no one tell me what she sings? —
Perhaps the plaintive numbers flow*
For old, unhappy, far-off things,
And battles long ago:
Or is it some more humble lay,*
Familiar matter of to-day?
Some natural sorrow, loss, or pain,
That has been, and may be again?

Whate'er the theme, the Maiden sang
As if her song could have no ending;
I saw her singing at her work,
And o'er the sickle bending; —
I listened, motionless and still;
And, as I mounted up the hill,
The music in my heart I bore,
Long after it was heard no more.

                                        William Wordsworth

Notes for **"The World Is Too Much With Us"**

This sonnet, written in 1806, argues that people are no longer moved by or impressed by nature; rather they are consumed by "...getting and spending." The poet would rather be a pagan who, looking at nature, would at least be reminded of the mythical sea gods Triton (a kind of merman) and Proteus (the original "old man of the sea"). Ask yourself if you are moved more by some latest gadget or convenience or more dumbstruck by a double-rainbow, a shooting star or a thundering rainstorm?

Compare this with Gerard Manly Hopkins' sonnet "God's Grandeur" also in this collection.

William Wordsworth (1770~1850), an English poet known for his worship of nature and love of humanity, was a leader of a movement called Romanticism that emphasized writing about imagination and emotion over intellect and reason (Classicism). Poetry for Wordsworth was "emotion recollected in tranquility." Writing at the opening of the nineteenth century Wordsworth, like many other poets, was appalled by the spreading industrial revolution and the rise, even then, of what we today call "consumerism." His close friends were Samuel Taylor Coleridge, John Keats, and Percy Bysshe Shelly. Wordsworth believed in democracy and the French Revolution (1789~1799). He was appointed Poet Laureate of England in 1843.

Most of Wordsworth's best known poetry is collected in *Lyrical Ballads with a Few Other Poems* (1798), which he published jointly with Samuel Coleridge.

**"Getting and spending,
   we lay waste our powers;...."**

The World is Too Much With Us

The world is too much with us; late and soon,
Getting and spending, we lay waste our powers;–
Little we see in Nature that is ours;
We have given our hearts away, a sordid boon!
The Sea that bares her bosom to the moon;
The winds that will be howling at all hours,
And are up-gathered now like sleeping flowers;
For this, for everything, we are out of tune;
It moves us not. Great God! I'd rather be
A Pagan suckled in a creed outworn;
So might I, standing on this pleasant lea,
Have glimpses that would make me less forlorn;
Have sight of Proteus rising from the sea;
Or hear old Triton blow his wreathed horn.

William Wordsworth

Notes for **"Composed on Westminster Bridge"**

This poem was written about the poet's morning trip through London with his sister Dorothy on their way to board a ship for Calais. Wordsworth sympathized with the French Revolution which was then taking place. Also, he was in love with a lady in France. Does this contribute to the mood of the poem?

This is a sonnet in the Petrarchan style. Usually in this kind of sonnet the last six lines present a solution or a commentary on the first eight lines. Does the poet follow that pattern? Or is it all simply in praise of a London morning? Dorothy said that the morning view of London from the bridge "was like one of Nature's own grand spectacles."

But is that *really* all the poem means?

Notice the word, "smokeless." The air is smokeless before the factories start working in the morning. Where every word matters, why would the poet use the word "smokeless"? Might this be a commentary on the "mighty heart" of the industrial revolution, that is, the rise of the factories? Note, amidst the morning silence of this usually busy city, what sole entity continues its course.

Compare this to William Blake's poem "Jerusalem" written in 1804, just two years later, where Blake complains about the "dark satanic mills" that are ruining the countryside. Contrast these churning "dark satanic mills" with the movement of the River Thames in Wordsworth's sonnet here.

Is the poem really about what London *ought* to be at all times?

William Wordsworh (1770~1850) was an English poet known for his worship of nature. He tried to write in "the language really used by men." He was appointed Poet Laureate of England in 1843.

**"This City now doth, like a garment, wear
The beauty of the morning; silent, bare, …."**

Composed on Westminster Bridge,
September 3, 1802

Earth has not anything to show more fair:
Dull would he be of soul who could pass by
A sight so touching in its majesty:
This City now doth, like a garment, wear
The beauty of the morning; silent, bare,
Ships, towers, domes, theatres, and temples lie
Open unto the fields, and to the sky;
All bright and glittering in the smokeless air.
Never did sun more beautifully steep
In his first splendour, valley, rock, or hill;
Ne'er saw I, never felt, a calm so deep!
The river glideth at his own sweet will:
Dear God! the very houses seem asleep;
And all that mighty heart is lying still!

William Wordsworth

Notes for **"Marmion"**

This memorable line: "Oh, what a tangled web we weave, When first we practise to deceive!" — often erroneously attributed to William Shakespeare — actually appears in lines 530-537 of Canto VI, Stanza XVII of Sir Walter Scott's long narrative poem, *Marmion: A Tale of Flodden Field* (for an explanation of how to convert Roman numerals to Arabic numerals, see p. 186 in this collection).

The poem, which runs for several thousand lines, tells a story about the fictional characters, Lord Marmion (a favorite of King Henry VIII), Sir Ralph de Wilton, and de Wilton's fiancée Clara de Clare whom Marmion wants to marry. The subplot that leads to these lines involves Marmion, who, with the help of a nun, Constance, who loves him, forges a letter that implicates de Wilton in committing treason. Among many, many other complications, Constance is then discovered to have broken her vows by cooperating with Marmion, and for that transgression is walled up alive in the convent. Marmion is discovered to have set up the plot and speaks these words in Canto VI.

There are many other plots and subplots, slanders and trickery, struggles and fighting, all set during the 1513 Battle of Flodden Field when the Scots attempted to invade England. The English finally won, and Marmion was killed in battle.

The poem is written mostly in rhymed couplets, sometimes in iambic pentameter, but often in iambic tetrameter and other measures. On occasion, Scott varies the rhymed couplets with other rhyme schemes in this long, narrative poem.

Sir Walter Scott (1771~1832) was a Scottish poet and novelist. His most well-known poem is *The Lay of the Last Minstrel,* ("lay" means a song). He is mostly remembered for historical novels, such as *Ivanhoe, Kenilworth, Waverley, Rob Roy* and *Guy Mannering.*

**"Oh, what a tangled web we weave,
When first we practise to deceive!"**

Marmion

Canto VI (The Battle) Stanza XVII

Canto VI   Stanza XVII
(Marmion speaking)

**** *first 24 lines of stanza XVII omitted*

"Yet Clare's sharp questions must I shun;
Must separate Constance from the nun -
Oh, what a tangled web we weave,
When first we practise to deceive!
A Palmer too! — no wonder why
I felt rebuked beneath his eye:
I might have known there was but one
Whose look could quell Lord Marmion."

Sir Walter Scott

Notes for **"Patriotism"**

This passage is the first part of Canto VI of *The Lay of the Last Minstrel,* a long narrative poem written in 1805 by Sir Walter Scott, that combines a love story, a family feud, and a border war.

This part of the poem, often called "Patriotism," uses a reverse form of praising those who love their country by criticizing and belittling those who do not love their "native land."

Sir Walter Scott, in his preface to the poem, wrote that the poem was "...intended to illustrate the customs and manners which anciently prevailed on the borders of England and Scotland," adding "...the Poem was put into the mouth of an ancient Minstrel, the last of the race, who, as he is supposed to have survived the Revolution, might have caught somewhat of the refinement of modern poetry, without losing the simplicity of his original model. The date of the Tale itself is about the middle of the sixteenth century, when most of the personages actually flourished. The time occupied by the action is Three Nights and Three Days."

Sir Walter Scott (1771~1832) was a Scottish poet and novelist concerned with patriotism, chivalry and pageantry. His most famous poems are *The Lay of the Last Minstrel* written in 1805, "Marmion" (1808) featuring the hero Lochinvar, and "The Lady of the Lake" (1810). Scott is mostly remembered for writing historical novels set in Scotland and England, such as *Ivanhoe, Kenilworth, Waverly, Guy Mannering, Rob Roy*, and *Quentin Durwood.*

"…Unwept, unhonor'd and unsung."

Patriotism
(excerpt from Canto VI of *The Lay of the Last Minstrel*)

Breathes there the man, with soul so dead,
Who never to himself hath said,
This is my own, my native land!
Whose heart hath ne'er within him burn'd,
As home his footsteps he hath turn'd,
From wandering on a foreign strand!
If such there breathe, go, mark him well;
For him no Minstrel raptures swell;
High though his titles, proud his name,
Boundless his wealth as wish can claim;
Despite those titles, power, and pelf,
The wretch, concentred all in self,
Living, shall forfeit fair renown,
And, doubly dying, shall go down
To the vile dust, from whence he sprung,
Unwept, unhonor'd, and unsung.

Sir Walter Scott

Notes for **"Kubla Khan"**

The poet Samuel Taylor Coleridge was taking opium for a dysentery condition and fell asleep while reading Samuel Purchas' *Purchas his Pilgrims*. Purchas' book, written in 1614, was inspired by the stories of Venetian explorer Marco Polo about the Mongolian Emperor, Kubla(i) Khan, who in 1264 built a beautiful marble castle in Xanadu (Shangdu, China).

When he awoke Coleridge recalled a dream and penned the first thirty lines of "Kubla Khan" before being interrupted by other business. He later added the twenty-four line second stanza.

In the first stanza. after a description of from Xanadu and Khan's "pleasure-dome," Coleridge quickly, with four lines of iambic tetrameter and end-rhyme, places the reader on the river Alph, flowing through "measureless" savage and chaotic caverns that adjoin the paradise. But the chaos interrupts the river only "momently." The river then resumes its flow through wood and dale down to "caverns measureless to man." In the final two lines of the first stanza Kubla Khan hears "from far / Ancestral voices prophesying war!"

In the second stanza the poet tells us that the pleasure dome is "sunny" with "caves of ice," and it, or at least its shadow, floats on the waves. But, a bit ominously, the noise from the fountains and the caves can still be heard. Perhaps Coleridge implies that the threat of war and chaos are always present, even though beauty is on the surface.

"In Xanadu did Kubla Khan...."

"...caverns measureless to man,...."

Kubla Khan:
Or,
A Vision In A Dream. A Fragment.

In Xanadu did Kubla Khan
A stately pleasure-dome decree:
Where Alph, the sacred river, ran
Through caverns measureless to man
Down to a sunless sea.
So twice five miles of fertile ground
With walls and towers were girdled round:
And there were gardens bright with sinuous rills,
Where blossomed many an incense-bearing tree;
And here were forests ancient as the hills,
Enfolding sunny spots of greenery.
But oh! that deep romantic chasm which slanted
Down the green hill athwart a cedarn cover!
A savage place! as holy and enchanted
As e'er beneath a waning moon was haunted
By woman wailing for her demon-lover!
And from this chasm, with ceaseless turmoil seething,
As if this earth in fast thick pants were breathing,
A mighty fountain momently was forced:
Amid whose swift half-intermitted burst
Huge fragments vaulted like rebounding hail,
Or chaffy grain beneath the thresher's flail:
And 'mid these dancing rocks at once and ever
It flung up momently the sacred river.
Five miles meandering with a mazy motion
Through wood and dale the sacred river ran,
Then reached the caverns measureless to man,
And sank in tumult to a lifeless ocean;
And 'mid this tumult Kubla heard from far
Ancestral voices prophesying war!

Notes for **"Kubla Khan"** (cont.)

Nevertheless, the poet writes that if he could revive his vision of a song by a damsel with a dulcimer, singing about Mount Abora, he would be so delighted he himself could build that pleasure dome. Some scholars think that Mount Abora refers to Mount Amara, which John Milton mentions in his poem "Paradise Lost," as one of the beautiful places in the world that could be compared to the biblical Garden of Eden.

In the last lines of the poem, some believe the poet suggests if he builds the beautiful "pleasure dome" floating in air with "caves of ice," people will say 'Beware, beware," watch out for this guy; he has power.'

Samuel Taylor Coleridge (1772~1834) and his good friend William Wordsworth were part of a group of the great English Romantic poets including John Keats, Percy Bysshe Shelley, Lord Byron, and Sir Walter Scott who lived and wrote at the end of the eighteenth and beginning of the nineteenth centuries. Coleridge was also known as a great critic. His three best known poems are "Kubla Khan," "Christabel" and, of course, *The Rime of the Ancient Mariner.*

The shadow of the dome of pleasure
Floated midway on the waves;
Where was heard the mingled measure
From the fountain and the caves.
It was a miracle of rare device,
A sunny pleasure-dome with caves of ice!

A damsel with a dulcimer
In a vision once I saw:
It was an Abyssinian maid,
And on her dulcimer she played,
Singing of Mount Abora.
Could I revive within me
Her symphony and song,
To such a deep delight 'twould win me,
That with music loud and long,
I would build that dome in air,
That sunny dome! those caves of ice!
And all who heard should see them there,
And all should cry, Beware! Beware!
His flashing eyes, his floating hair!
Weave a circle round him thrice,
And close your eyes with holy dread,
For he on honey-dew hath fed,
And drunk the milk of Paradise.

Samuel Taylor Coleridge

Notes for *The Rime of the Ancient Mariner*

These are excerpts from a 626-line poem, *The Rime of the Ancient Mariner*, one of the most famous poems in the English language. *The Rime of the Ancient Mariner* was both first published in 1798 and again in final form in 1817 with Coleridge's marginal notes. The poem is in ballad form with one-hundred-seven of the 142 stanzas in regular four-line form (four feet, three feet, four feet, three feet, with a rhyme scheme of a-b-c-b). The other stanzas range from five to nine lines.

The story is simple: sailing on a ship, the mariner, for a reason we do not know, has broken the law of loving all creatures great and small by killing an albatross, the bird that has led the ship out of the South Pole sea ice. The mariner then has to carry that guilt (the albatross around his neck) that also dooms the rest of the crew until he shows his love by blessing the water snakes. Then the albatross falls off his neck. As much as the moral at the end about love, the poem also tries to show that there are consequences for bad acts. In addition, reading Herman Melville's epic novel *Moby Dick* will allow readers to further explore a more developed version (with different outcome) of this poem's main theme.

The reader has to pay close attention in reading the poem because the main characters, the narrator, the wedding guest and the mariner, interrupt each other and sometimes it is hard to discern who is speaking if one just breezes through the poem. Also the pilot, the pilot's son, and the hermit (as well as two "voices") have speaking lines.

"Water, water every where, nor any drop to drink."

"…the Albatross / About my neck was hung."

**"He prayeth best, who loveth best
All things both great and small;…."**

The Rime of the Ancient Mariner
***** = omitted lines

Opening lines from **Part I**

It is an ancient Mariner,
And he stoppeth one of three.
'By thy long grey beard and glittering eye,
Now wherefore stopp'st thou me?

*(The Mariner accosts a wedding guest and tells the guest
both how, on a voyage south of the equator, the Mariner
killed an albatross and how subsequent evils then beset
his ship.)*

from **Part II**
*****

Water, water, every where,
And all the boards did shrink;
Water, water, every where,
Nor any drop to drink.
*****

Ah! well a-day! what evil looks
Had I from old and young!
Instead of the cross, the Albatross
About my neck was hung.

Notes for **"The Rime of the Ancient Mariner"**
(cont.)

Samuel Taylor Coleridge (1772~1834) and his good friend William Wordsworth were part of the great English Romantic poet group of poets, which included John Keats, Percy Bysshe Shelley, Lord Byron, and Sir Walter Scott who all lived and wrote at the end of the eighteenth and beginning of the nineteenth centuries. Coleridge was also known as a great critic. His three best known poems are "Christabel," "Kubla Khan," and *The Rime of the Ancient Mariner*.

from **Part VII**

*****

Farewell, farewell! this I tell
To thee, thou Wedding-Guest!
He prayeth well, who loveth well
Both man and bird and beast.

He prayeth best, who loveth best
All things both great and small;
For the dear God who loveth us,
He made and loveth all.
*****

Samuel Taylor Coleridge

Notes for **"Abou Ben Adhem"**

The opening line "Abou Ben Adhem (may his tribe increase)" is often quoted as a reference to a person who loves his fellow man.

Leigh Hunt (1784~1859) was an English journalist, editor, publisher of *The Examiner*, and poet. He wrote "Abou Ben Adhem" in 1834. Leigh Hunt was also an insightful literary critic, who discovered and introduced many poets to the public, including Robert Browning, John Keats, Percy Bysshe Shelley, and Alfred Tennyson. John Keats and Perce Bysshe Shelley became Leigh Hunt's close friends. Leigh Hunt was considered a second-tier Romantic poet, with his most prolific period of poetical activity being between 1812~1820.

"Abou Ben Adhem (may his tribe increase!)"

Abou Ben Adhem

Abou Ben Adhem (may his tribe increase!)
Awoke one night from a deep dream of peace,
And saw, within the moonlight in his room,
Making it rich, and like a lily in bloom,
An angel writing in a book of gold: —
Exceeding peace had made Ben Adhem bold,
And to the presence in the room he said
"What writest thou?" — The vision raised its head,
And with a look made of all sweet accord,
Answered "The names of those who love the Lord."
"And is mine one?" said Abou. "Nay, not so,"
Replied the angel. Abou spoke more low,
But cheerly still, and said "I pray thee, then,
Write me as one that loves his fellow men."

The angel wrote, and vanished. The next night
It came again with a great wakening light,
And showed the names whom love of God had blest,
And lo! Ben Adhem's name led all the rest.

Leigh Hunt

Notes for **"Jenny Kissed Me"**

This short, exuberant poem, a favorite of many, was first published in November, 1838.

In 1835 Leigh Hunt and his large family moved to Chelsea in London and became neighbor to poet and author Thomas Carlyle at Carlyle's suggestion. The two became close friends and Hunt's home was always open to his circle of friends, of which there were many.

Two stories exist about the poem. One story is that Leigh Hunt visited the Carlyle house to deliver the news that he was going to publish one of Thomas Carlyle's poems. When the news was delivered to Carlyle's wife, Jane, she jumped up and kissed him. The other story is that during one winter Leigh Hunt was sick with influenza and absent for so long that when he finally recovered and went to visit the Carlyles, Jane jumped up and kissed him as soon as he appeared at the door. Two days later one of the Hunt servants delivered a note addressed, "From Mr. Hunt to Mrs. Carlyle." It contained the poem "Jenny Kissed Me."

Leigh Hunt (1784~1859) was an English journalist and poet. He wrote his famous poem, "Abou Ben Adhem," in 1834. He was a friend of Shelley, Keats and Lord Byron.

> "Say I'm growing old, but add,
> Jenny kiss'd me."

Jenny Kiss'd Me

Jenny kiss'd me when we met,
  Jumping from the chair she sat in;
Time, you thief, who love to get
  Sweets into your list, put that in!
Say I'm weary, say I'm sad,
  Say that health and wealth have missed me,
Say I'm growing old, but add,
  Jenny kiss'd me.

Leigh Hunt

Notes for **"She Walks in Beauty"**

This poem was written, according to legend, in response to the poet seeing his cousin Lady Wilmot Horton at a funeral in a mourning dress on June 11th, 1814.

One might think this to be a love poem, but the poet does not clearly state he loves the lady he is writing about. The poet merely describes her beauty, uses the contrast of dark and light in his description, and suggests that, like the stars in a clear sky, the lady has the best of dark and light, a beauty higher than what would be seen by day. So tender is her balanced beauty, even the slightest adjustment would change the vision. The poet then considers how this beauty reflects her goodness and then her innocence. The theme of the poem is similar to that of Wordsworth's perspective in *The Solitary Reaper* (p. 107 in this collection), that is, merely contemplating the beauty of the woman he sees.

The poem is in a rhythm known as <u>iambic tetrameter</u>, a kind of verse preferred by Byron and many, many other poets:

An **iamb** = a two-syllable 'foot': usually an unaccented and unstressed first syllable, followed by an accented and stressed second syllable. Analogous to a single heartbeat, single skipping step, or the single gallop of a horse in full cantor, one **iamb**, said aloud, might sound like ***da-dúm***.

Tetrameter = four meters, or four iambs:
one 'foot' X 4.

Said aloud:
  da-dúm *da-dúm* *da-dúm* *da-dúm*
So: **She walks / in beau / ty, like / the night**
or

One shade / the more, /one ray / the less,

For Lord Byron's biography, see his next poem
"We'll No More Go a Roving."

"She walks in beauty, like the night...."

She Walks in Beauty

She walks in beauty, like the night
Of cloudless climes and starry skies;
And all that's best of dark and bright
Meet in her aspect and her eyes:
Thus mellowed to that tender light
Which heaven to gaudy day denies.

One shade the more, one ray the less,
Had half impaired the nameless grace
Which waves in every raven tress,
Or softly lightens o'er her face;
Where thoughts serenely sweet express,
How pure, how dear their dwelling-place.

And on that cheek, and o'er that brow,
So soft, so calm, yet eloquent,
The smiles that win, the tints that glow,
But tell of days in goodness spent,
A mind at peace with all below,
A heart whose love is innocent!

Lord Byron, George Gordon

Notes for **"We'll Go No More a Roving"**

This poem was written in Venice (a city that Byron loved) in 1817. However, it was not published until 1830, six years after his death.

Lord Byron was only twenty-nine when he wrote this poem, a seeming lament on aging. A consummate traveler, romantic, adventurer (in 1810 he purportedly [like the Greek hero Leander] swam across the Hellespont, a somewhat treacherous four-mile strait in Turkey now called "the Dardanelles"), and early wearer of the open-neck shirt, Byron's verse here alludes to his tiring of the wild and high life, addressing mortality: the "sword outwears its sheath" and "soul wears out the breast." Concurrently, he realizes, at this stage of his life, more serious pursuits were worth his attention.

A majority of Lord Byron's poetry originates from an informed self-analysis during revolutionary times, and he proclaims in Canto XV of *Don Juan*: "I was born for opposition," a phrase harkening back to the literary aspirations of Francois Voltaire, Miguel de Cervantes, and Alexander Pope, all of whom influenced Byron.

He wrote *Don Juan* and many of his most important poems during the seven years following this poem and before he died at age thirty-six. A consummate humanitarian and forever in opposition to social injustices, tyranny, and hypocrisy, Lord Byron even foresaw his own 'revolutionary' campaigns continuing posthumously in Canto IV of *Childe Harold*:

> "**But I have lived, and have not lived in vain**:
> My mind may lose its force, my blood its fire,
> And my frame perish even in conquering pain,
> But there is that within me which shall tire
> Torture and Time, and breathe when I expire [.]"

"We'll go no more a roving...."

So We'll Go No More a Roving

So, we'll go no more a roving
   So late into the night,
Though the heart be still as loving,
   And the moon be still as bright.

For the sword outwears its sheath,
   And the soul wears out the breast,
And the heart must pause to breathe,
   And love itself have rest.

Though the night was made for loving,
   And the day returns too soon,
Yet we'll go no more a roving
   By the light of the moon.

Lord Byron (George Gordon)

Lord Byron (1788~1824), George Gordon Byron, was the 6th Baron Byron of Rochdale and was known simply as "Lord Byron." He was an English poet of the Romantic Movement (like Wordsworth, Coleridge, Shelley and Keats – yet far less insular) who wrote many poems. His best-known verse chronicles romantic heroes who performed heroic deeds; lives he often attempted to live out himself. *Childe Harold* and *Don Juan* are just two of these. He lived a rather wild life, and because of both his somewhat tempestuous reputation and surmounting debt, moved to Switzerland, then to Italy, and then finally onto Greece, where he petitioned internationally and fought domestically (financing a small, international, private militia known as 'Byron's Brigade') to secure Greece's independence from the Ottoman Empire, being proclaimed a "national hero" by Greece at the time of his death.

Notes for **"Ozymandias"**

The sonnet "Ozymandias" is Percy Bysshe Shelley's best-known short poem. The argument of the poem is that despite the fact a frowning and sneering king had a statue erected to honor himself so those of future generations would "look on my works" and despair of ever being as great, now future generations can both see only that "nothing beside remains" and that the statue is now a decayed, colossal wreck. The poem tells us about the impermanence of physical things, especially the transitory nature of empire and political power; here the power of kings.

Ozymandias, or more commonly known as Rameses II, was a great pharaoh of Egypt. His visage was depicted (or "mocked" or 'replicated' here) by the sculptor, who too, like many other citizens, must have lived and/or "fed" off of such a massive project, which ordered by Ozymandias, provided work and sustenance for the masses. Surviving depictions of Rameses II, however, reveal the pharaoh's face to have a slightly playful expression, and so Ozymandias' "wrinkled lip and sneer of cold command" here reveal more about the author's opposition to tyrannical power — Shelley's own 'sculpting' and replication of the traveller's words.

Note how Shelley's use of imagery starts vertically with a statue whose legs still "stand," moves to a "shattered visage" that lies "half sunk," and then finishes horizontally with "lone and level sands" that "stretch far away." The "pedestal" at the beginning of the final sestet (six lines) not only serves as a fulcrum for moving the vertical statue horizontally into the "boundless and bare" but also reminds the reader of what happens to any entity that is 'put on a pedestal.'

Percy Bysshe Shelley (1792~1822) is generally thought of as one of the finest English lyric poets during the Romantic Period. Although he wrote some novels, he is best known for his poems about beauty, liberty, and freedom. He was married to Mary Shelley who wrote the novel *Frankenstein*.

"Look on my works, ye mighty, and despair!"

Ozymandias

I met a traveller from an antique land
Who said— "Two vast and trunkless legs of stone
Stand in the desert.... Near them on the sand,
Half sunk, a shattered visage lies, whose frown,
And wrinkled lip and sneer of cold command,
Tell that its sculptor well those passions read
Which yet survive, stamped on these lifeless things,
The hand that mocked them and the heart that fed;
And on the pedestal these words appear:
My name is Ozymandias, King of Kings:
Look on my works, ye mighty, and despair!
Nothing beside remains. Round the decay
Of that colossal wreck, boundless and bare,
The lone and level sands stretch far away."

Percy Bysshe Shelley

Notes for **"Casabianca"**

This poem commemorates an actual incident that occurred in 1798 during the "Battle of the Nile" between the British under Admiral Nelson and the French ship *Orient* commanded by Louis de Casabianca.

During the battle the French Commander, mortally wounded, lay on the lower deck of his ship. As night approached the ship was on fire, and Nelson ordered his men to rescue the officers and crew. All the Frenchmen debarked except the boy, Giocante Casabianca, who refused to go, saying that his father had told him not to leave the ship, and that he could not disobey that order. Shortly thereafter the flames reached the stored gunpowder and the ship exploded.

As the poet's use of iambic tetrameter and *abab* rhyme scheme moves the reader feverishly and quickly through the verses, note the beautiful boy's steadfast resolve amidst the terrible and imminently dangerous circumstances. Compare the acceleration in this poem with Earnest Lawrence Thayer's "Casey at the Bat" later in this collection.

This poem was in McGuffey's Fourth Reader (1866) and was a recital piece in elementary schools in England and the United States from the 1870s through the 1950s.

"The boy stood on the burning deck...."

Casabianca

The boy stood on the burning deck
    Whence all but he had fled;
The flame that lit the battle's wreck
    Shone round him o'er the dead.

Yet beautiful and bright he stood,
    As born to rule the storm -
A creature of heroic blood,
    A proud, though child-like form.

The flames rolled on - he would not go
    Without his Father's word;
That father, faint in death below,
    His voice no longer heard.

He called aloud: – "Say, Father, say
    If yet my task is done?"
He knew not that the chieftain lay
    Unconscious of his son.

"Speak, father!" once again he cried,
    "If I may yet be gone!"
And but the booming shots replied,
    And fast the flames rolled on.

Notes for **"Casabianca"** (cont.)

Felicia Dorothea Browne Hemans (1793~1835) was a British poet born in Liverpool, who after her husband left her in 1818, supported herself and her five sons by writing poetry. She died in Dublin, Ireland in 1835.

Upon his brow he felt their breath,
    And in his waving hair,
And looked from that lone post of death
    In still yet brave despair;

And shouted but once more aloud,
    "My father! must I stay?"
While o'er him fast, through sail and shroud,
    The wreathing fires made way.

They wrapt the ship in splendour wild,
    They caught the flag on high,
And streamed above the gallant child,
    Like banners in the sky.

There came a burst of thunder-sound-
    The boy – oh where was he
Ask of the winds that far around
    With fragments strewed the sea!

With mast, and helm, and pennon fair,
    That well had borne their part –
But the noblest thing which perished there
    Was that young faithful heart.

Felicia Dorothea Browne Hemans

Notes for *Endymion*

* **bower** = a leafy shelter or rustic cottage
* **wreathing** = weaving into a wreath
* **spite** = in spite of
* **pall** = shadow
* **Such** = "such as" or "for example"
* **boon** = a gift, a goodness (the trees provide shade)
* **rills** = small streams
* **brake** = a forest thicket
* **dooms** = the after-life

This is the opening stanza of a 5000-line poem by John Keats about the myth of the handsome shepherd, Endymion, who seeks to fall in love with Cynthia, the goddess of the moon. Yet Endymion eventually realizes that an earthly Indian maiden is his true love. The poem was not well received by literary critics, and except for these opening lines, hardly anyone ever reads it.

The poem is best understood by noting the punctuation and not stopping at the end of each line. Note how Keats refers to cycles of movement: the "circle of life," and how nature continually provides sustenance and shelter.

John Keats (1795~1821) was an English poet, a friend of William Wordsworth and Percy Bysshe Shelley, and together these three were the most famous poets of the Romantic Movement. Although trained to be a surgeon and was licensed in 1816 as an apothecary, Keats instead decided on writing poetry and, in the five years before his death, produced many very beautiful poems. John Keats was a master in his conveyance of visual imagery in and through written verse, and his expression of natural beauty is unparalleled in the history of poetry. His first poem was a sonnet called "On First Looking into Chapman's Homer" (1816), and it made him famous. Later in 1818 he wrote "Ode on a Grecian Urn," *Endymion,* "La Belle Dame Sans Merci," and "The Eve of St. Agnes," among many others.

"A thing of beauty is a joy for ever:...."

from *Endymion*
(excerpt from Book I)

A thing of beauty is a joy for ever:
Its loveliness increases; it will never
Pass into nothingness; but still will keep
A bower quiet for us, and a sleep*
Full of sweet dreams, and health, and quiet breathing.
Therefore, on every morrow, are we wreathing*
A flowery band to bind us to the earth,
Spite of despondence, of the inhuman dearth*
Of noble natures, of the gloomy days,
Of all the unhealthy and o'er-darkened ways
Made for our searching: yes, in spite of all,
Some shape of beauty moves away the pall*
From our dark spirits. Such the sun, the moon,*
Trees old and young, sprouting a shady boon*
For simple sheep; and such are daffodils
With the green world they live in; and clear rills*
That for themselves a cooling covert make
'Gainst the hot season; the mid-forest brake*
Rich with a sprinkling of fair musk-rose blooms:
And such too is the grandeur of the dooms*
We have imagined for the mighty dead;
An endless fountain of immortal drink,
Pouring unto us from the heaven's brink.

John Keats

Notes for
"On First Looking Into Chapman's Homer"

* **western islands** = islands in the Mediterranean
* **bards in fealty to Apollo hold** = poets have said that the Greek gods rule the Mediterranean islands
* **one wide expanse... that deep browed Homer ruled as his demesne** = a sea that the Greek poet Homer wrote about extensively
* **pure serene** = bright sky, pure air
* **Chapman's Homer** = George Chapman (1559~1634) was an English poet whose most notable achievement was his translations of Homer's poems *The Iliad* and *The Odyssey*. Chapman's translations were praised by many poets of the time.
* **stout Cortez** = John Keats makes an error here. It was Balboa, not Cortez, who first discovered the Pacific Ocean.
* **Darien** = Darien province in Panama

Despite of his wide and worldly experience, the poet realizes that he did not fully appreciate the world that Homer described in *The Iliad* and *The Odyssey* until reading George Chapman's translations. He compares his feelings on reading these translations to the feeling of discovering a new planet or to discovering the Pacific Ocean.

This poem is a sonnet, and as such, presents a problem and a solution. The problem at hand, of course, is Keats' limited understanding of Homer, with the solution being how listening to Chapman's translations brought a new, vast interpretation into Keats' world view — his "ken":

> *Then felt I like some watcher of the skies*
> *When a new planet swims into his ken...*

"Silent, upon a peak in Darien."

On First Looking into Chapman's Homer

Much have I travell'd in the realms of gold,
And many goodly states and kingdoms seen;
Round many western islands have I been*
Which bards in fealty to Apollo hold.*
Oft of one wide expanse had I been told
That deep-brow'd Homer ruled as his demesne;*
Yet did I never breathe its pure serene*
Till I heard Chapman speak out loud and bold:*
Then felt I like some watcher of the skies
When a new planet swims into his ken;
Or like stout Cortez when with eagle eyes*
He star'd at the Pacific — and all his men
Look'd at each other with a wild surmise —
Silent, upon a peak in Darien.*

John Keats

John Keats (1795~1821) was an English poet, who lost both parents at an early age: his father trampled by a horse when John Keats was eight; his mother dying of tuberculosis, which would later take John Keats' own life at the young age of twenty-five. He drew comfort from these personal tragedies through his continued studies in art and literature. Eventually, Keats was introduced by a friend to the rather radical yet influential editor and literary critic Leigh Hunt (see p. 124), who not only introduced Keats to politics but also to the other two great Romantic Movement poets William Wordsworth and Percy Bysshe Shelley. This sonnet (Keats' first) made him famous, and following Hunt's subsequent imprisonment for libeling the Prince Regent, Keats praises Hunt in yet another sonnet entitled "Written on the Day that Mr. Leigh Hunt Left Prison." Though these sonnets are Italian/Petrarchan in form, John Keats also experimented with the Shakespearean sonnet form in his "When I Have Fears That I May Cease to Be." For a review of sonnet forms see pages 48-49 in this collection.

Notes for **"Concord Hymn"**

This poem "Concord Hymn" by Ralph Waldo Emerson was written for the dedication of the Concord Monument on April 19, 1836 to commemorate the Revolutionary War battle at Concord Bridge on April 19, 1775.

The famous line from this poem is "…fired the shot heard round the world." Those words are often used these days to refer to other great events.

It would be good to commit to memory the first stanza of this poem both to know the source of the line and to remember the time and place of the first battle of the American Revolution.

This poem is not one of Emerson's best poems, but it does contain that memorable line.

Ralph Waldo Emerson (1803~1882), according to Yale professor Harold Bloom, "…is the mind of America." What matters most, said Bloom, are "…his prose writings: essays, lectures, notebooks and journals." After graduation from Harvard in 1817 and then Harvard Divinity School, Emerson became a Unitarian minister. But in 1832 he resigned his ministry, and after a visit to England and Scotland, he returned to New England to become a writer and lecturer, becoming famous after his 1838 Harvard Divinity School address. Emerson's most quoted essay is "Self Reliance." He was a mentor to Henry David Thoreau and Walt Whitman among many others and a friend of Henry Wadsworth Longfellow. Professor Bloom says that "…after Walt Whitman and Emily Dickinson, Emerson is the most considerable poet of the nineteenth century in the United States."

RALPH WALDO EMERSON

"...fired the shot heard round the world."

Concord Hymn

By the rude bridge that arched the flood,
   Their flag to April's breeze unfurled,
Here once the embattled farmers stood
   And fired the shot heard round the world.

The foe long since in silence slept;
   Alike the conqueror silent sleeps;
And Time the ruined bridge has swept
   Down the dark stream which seaward creeps.

On this green bank, by this soft stream,
   We set today a votive stone;
That memory may their deed redeem,
   When, like our sires, our sons are gone.

Spirit, that made those heroes dare
   To die, and leave their children free,
Bid Time and Nature gently spare
   The shaft we raise to them and thee.

Ralph Waldo Emerson

Notes for **"Sonnets from the Portuguese No. 43"**

Published first in 1850, the forty-four poems that became *Sonnets from the Portuguese* were written by Elizabeth Barrett between 1845 and 1846, while both she and the poet Robert Browning were courting. Browning often called her "my little Portuguese;" hence the title of the collection. Sonnet 43 "How Do I Love Thee?" is the second to last of these sonnets and is considered one of the greatest expressions of romantic love.

The poet begins this sonnet with a question to herself and answers with the involvement of her total being. Her sonnet's question and answer almost challenge the reader to question whether or not such a love is possible in her/his own lifetime — and then beyond! Moreover, note the uniformity of the *eight* lines of end-rhyme following the question, and then compare the alternating end-rhyme scheme of the last *six* lines.

How does this affect your reading of the sonnet?

Elizabeth Barrett Browning (1806~1861) was a self-educated English poet having read much of Shakespeare and Milton by the time she was in her early teens. Confined to her parent's home in London with a lung disease and a spine injury, she wrote poetry and in 1826 published her first volume: *An Essay on Mind and Other Poems.* In her 1844 collection entitled *Poems*, she praised the work of the poet Robert Browning, and Browning responded with a letter. At the time, Elizabeth was considered a more outstanding poet than Robert. The two began a correspondence and over the next six years exchanged nearly 600 letters. Against the wishes of her father, Elizabeth eloped with Browning in 1846, and they moved to Florence, Italy. Elizabeth Barrett Browning was both devoted to the classics and supported humanitarian causes, opposing slavery among other issues. She died in Italy in 1861.

"How do I love thee?"

Sonnets from the Portuguese
No. 43

How do I love thee? Let me count the ways.
I love thee to the depth and breadth and height
My soul can reach, when feeling out of sight
For the ends of being and ideal grace.
I love thee to the level of every day's
Most quiet need, by sun and candle-light.
I love thee freely, as men strive for right;
I love thee purely, as they turn from praise.
I love thee with the passion put to use
In my old griefs, and with my childhood's faith.
I love thee with a love I seemed to lose
With my lost saints. I love thee with the breath,
Smiles, tears, of all my life; and, if God choose,
I shall but love thee better after death.

Elizabeth Barrett Browning

Notes for **"A Psalm of Life"**

What is a psalm ? A sacred song or verse.

This poem reflects a *carpe diem* (Latin for "seize the day") view of life.

Apparently the poet is responding to another poet (a psalmist) who has in some poem ("mournful numbers" because poems were sometimes called "numbers") written that life on earth is just a dream; to trust in future rewards.

Longfellow counters, suggesting one makes meaning of (an impression on) any day and the world around her/him through one's in-the-moment inspirational labors and actions. His theme is similar to Edward FitzGerald's "The Rubaiyat of Omar Khayyam."

Take note of the thematic word-thread woven by Longfellow from the end of one verse to the beginning of the next verse:

"...not what they seem" ...> "Life is real!"
"...spoken of the soul-...> "Not enjoyment, and not sorrow,"
              "...farther....> "...long,..."
              "...marches ...> "...battle..."
              "...Be a hero ...> "...Trust no future,..."
              "...God...> "...great men..."
              "...Footprints... > Footprints..."
    "...shall take heart again....> "...be up and doing,...."

Finally, what do you think the poet's purpose was in both writing tomorrow as "to-morrow" and today as "to-day"?

"…things are not what they seem."
"Life is real! Life is earnest!"
"Art is long and Time is fleeting,…."
"…Footprints on the sands of time;…"

A Psalm of Life

What The Heart Of The Young Man
Said To The Psalmist.

Tell me not, in mournful numbers,
　　Life is but an empty dream!
For the soul is dead that slumbers,
　　And things are not what they seem.

Life is real! Life is earnest!
　　And the grave is not its goal;
Dust thou art, to dust returnest,
　　Was not spoken of the soul.

Not enjoyment, and not sorrow,
　　Is our destined end or way;
But to act, that each to-morrow
　　Find us farther than to-day.

Art is long, and Time is fleeting,
　　And our hearts, though stout and brave,
Still, like muffled drums, are beating
　　Funeral marches to the grave.

In the world's broad field of battle,
　　In the bivouac of Life,
Be not like dumb, driven cattle!
　　Be a hero in the strife!

Notes for **"A Psalm of Life"** (cont.)

Henry Wadsworth Longfellow (1807~1882) was a very popular American poet from New England in the 1800s and a professor of modern languages at Harvard. He wrote mostly long narrative poems such as *The Song of Hiawatha, Evangeline, The Courtship of Miles Standish,* and "The Landlord's Tale. Paul Revere's Ride."

Although he is sometimes now considered a lesser poet, until the mid-twentieth century Longfellow's poems recreating American history and myths were recited in classrooms throughout the United States. Longfellow is still said to have made one of the best translations into English of Dante's great poem *The Divine Comedy* and has given us many memorable phrases quoted today, some of which are in this collection. True to his calling as a professor of language, when he wrote a poem for the fiftieth anniversary of his class of 1825 at Bowdoin College, he resurrected a now often-quoted (and parodied) phrase from the works of the Roman historian Suetonius and entitled his poem, "Morituri Salutamus" ("…, we who are about to die, Salute you!"). The first quatrain gives us the whole historical story:

> **"O Caesar, we who are about to die**
> **Salute you!" was the gladiator's cry**
> **In the arena, standing face to face**
> **With death and with the Roman populace.**

Trust no Future, howe'er pleasant!
  Let the dead Past bury its dead!
Act, — act in the living Present!
  Heart within, and God o'erhead!

Lives of great men all remind us
  We can make our lives sublime,
And, departing, leave behind us
  Footprints on the sands of time;

Footprints, that perhaps another,
  Sailing o'er life's solemn main,
A forlorn and shipwrecked brother,
  Seeing, shall take heart again.

Let us, then, be up and doing,
  With a heart for any fate;
Still achieving, still pursuing,
  Learn to labor and to wait.

Henry Wadsworth Longfellow

Notes for *The Song of Hiawatha*

The Song of Hiawatha, written in 1855, is a very long narrative poem of twenty-two sections (each about 400 or more lines) that recounts the adventures of a Native American hero. The setting is on the southern shore of Lake Superior ('Gitche Gumee,' which in Ojibwa meant "Big Water"), where Hiawatha was reared among the Ojibwa tribe of Native Americans. The poem tells how Hiawatha brings progress and blessings to his tribe and helps create peace among the other tribes.

In this poem Longfellow weaves together many aspects of American Indian mythology concerning life, nature, and ritual, and tells of Hiawatha's many adventures and his marriage to Minnehaha, a beautiful maiden of the Dakota tribe.

This fragment is Section twenty-two, the last part of the poem (with many lines deleted *****) about the departure of Hiawatha. The deleted lines tell of the coming of the white Christian missionaries and Hiawatha's last message to his people to listen to the missionaries and treat them with kindness. This section may be viewed in many ways: for example, the author may be saying that Native Americans are in need of Christianity, or that Native Americans are welcoming to those who come over the brackish (salt) waters in ships with pinions (birds' wings = sails), or that this arrival of the white missionaries and the departure of Hiawatha symbolizes the end of Native American culture.

"By the shore of Gitche Gumee,...."
The Song of Hiawatha

(Part XXII. *Hiawatha's Departure*)

***** = lines omitted

By the shore of Gitche Gumee,
By the shining Big-Sea-Water,
At the doorway of his wigwam,
In the pleasant Summer morning,
Hiawatha stood and waited.
All the air was full of freshness,
All the earth was bright and joyous,
And before him, through the sunshine,
Westward toward the neighboring forest
Passed in golden swarms the Ahmo,
Passed the bees, the honey-makers,
Burning, singing in the sunshine.
  Bright above him shone the heavens,
Level spread the lake before him;
From its bosom leaped the sturgeon,
Sparkling, flashing in the sunshine;
*****

  Forth into the village went he,
Bade farewell to all the warriors,
Bade farewell to all the young men,
Spake persuading, spake in this wise:
  "I am going, O my people,
On a long and distant journey;
Many moons and many winters
Will have come, and will have vanished,
Ere I come again to see you...."
*****

  On the shore stood Hiawatha,
Turned and waved his hand at parting;
On the clear and luminous water
Launched his birch canoe for sailing,

Notes for *The Song of Hiawatha* (cont.)

These final lines of the poem give the reader a sense of how Longfellow tried to use rhythm to imitate Indian drums and chants. Think both of how Tennyson tried to imitate horses charging in the "Charge of the Light Brigade" and how Belloc attempted to imitate the rhythm of the *Tarantella* dance in his poem of the same name (pages 191 and 269 respectively in this collection).

Henry Wadsworth Longfellow (1807~1882), a popular and very well-read New England poet in the 1880s, was a professor of modern languages at Harvard. He wrote mostly narrative poems such as *The Song of Hiawatha, Evangeline, The Courtship of Miles Standish*, and "The Landlord's Tale. Paul Reverse's Ride."

From the pebbles of the margin
Shoved it forth into the water;
Whispered to it, "Westward! westward!"
And with speed it darted forward.
*****

Westward, westward Hiawatha
Sailed into the fiery sunset,
Sailed into the purple vapors,
Sailed into the dusk of evening:

  And the people from the margin
Watched him floating, rising, sinking,
Till the birch canoe seemed lifted
High into that sea of splendor,
Till it sank into the vapors
Like the new moon slowly, slowly
Sinking in the purple distance.

  And they said, "Farewell forever!"
Said, "Farewell, O Hiawatha!"
And the forests, dark and lonely,
Moved through all their depths of darkness,
Sighed, "Farewell, O Hiawatha!"
And the waves upon the margin
Rising, rippling on the pebbles,
Sobbed, "Farewell, O Hiawatha!"
And the heron, the Shuh-shuh-gah,
From her haunts among the fen-lands,
Screamed, "Farewell, O Hiawatha!"
  Thus departed Hiawatha,
Hiawatha the Beloved,
In the glory of the sunset,
In the purple mists of evening,
To the regions of the home-wind,
Of the Northwest-Wind, Keewaydin,
To the Islands of the Blessed,
To the Kingdom of Ponemah,
To the Land of the Hereafter!

Henry Wadsworth Longfellow

Notes for **"The Landlord's Tale."**

This poem, informally known as 'The Midnight Ride of Paul Revere,' is one of the poems included in Henry Wadsworth Longfellow's collection, *Tales of a Wayside Inn*. The idea of the collection was to bring together stories of persons who are staying at an Inn and tell tales to each other to pass the time. The most famous of the stories is "The Landlord's Tale. Paul Revere's Ride."

"The Landlord's Tale. Paul Revere's Ride" is a stirring poem, the whole of which is printed here. Commemorating the events of April 18, 1775, it was written in 1863 on the eve of the Civil War and was meant as a plea by Longfellow, an ardent abolitionist, to stir his friends in the north to action. He wanted to show how the actions of one man could affect history.

The poem, however, is full of historical inaccuracies. For example, Revere and several others rode out to warn that "The Regulars are coming" because "Regulars," not "British," is what the colonists would have called the troops. Revere was supplied with one of the fastest horses in Charleston, named Brown Beauty, and though he was able to outrace the British pursuing him, he did not ride "through the night." He rode first to Lexington where he warned Samuel Adams and John Hancock. There he was joined by two other riders, William Dawes and Dr. Samuel Prescott. When the three riders left Lexington for Concord, they were arrested by British troops. Prescott escaped and rode on to Concord, Dawes lost his horse and proceeded there on foot; Revere, however, did not escape. He was made captive, interrogated and then released. His horse was taken from him, and he never did reach Concord.

Thus, Revere did not act alone, nor did he ride through the night to Concord. But Revere did, in fact, through his many connections, arrange for the warning rides, he arranged for the signal lights, and he did indeed, silently and stealthily, cross to Charleston under the bow of British ships.

"One, if by land, and two, if by sea;
And I on the opposite shore will be,…"

The Landlord's Tale. Paul Revere's Ride

Listen, my children, and you shall hear
Of the midnight ride of Paul Revere,
On the eighteenth of April, in Seventy-five;
Hardly a man is now alive
Who remembers that famous day and year.

He said to his friend, "If the British march
By land or sea from the town to-night,
Hang a lantern aloft in the belfry arch
Of the North Church tower as a signal light, —
One, if by land, and two, if by sea;
And I on the opposite shore will be,
Ready to ride and spread the alarm
Through every Middlesex village and farm,
For the country folk to be up and to arm."
Then he said, "Good night!" and with muffled oar
Silently rowed to the Charlestown shore,
Just as the moon rose over the bay,
Where swinging wide at her moorings lay
The Somerset, British man-of-war;
A phantom ship, with each mast and spar
Across the moon like a prison bar,
And a huge black hulk, that was magnified
By its own reflection in the tide.

Meanwhile, his friend, through alley and street,
Wanders and watches with eager ears,
Till in the silence around him he hears
The muster of men at the barrack door,
The sound of arms, and the tramp of feet,
And the measured tread of the grenadiers,
Marching down to their boats on the shore.

Notes for **"The Landlord's Tale"** (cont.)

Historical anomalies notwithstanding, the poem's verses do display Longfellow's poetic powers of sound and sense ("Now soft on the sand, now loud on the ledge") and rhythm. Also, his figurative use of metaphorical language, often assigning human traits to otherwise inanimate entities (*personifying* them), enlivens both the verses and concurrently the reader's own 'ride' too through the poem (for more on extended metaphor and personification, see also Carl Sandburg's "Fog" on p. 293 and "The Grass" on p. 295 in this collection).

Hence, in addition to this poem's accelerating narrative tension between the ominous British fleet in the bay and Revere's impatience to mount and ride on the shore, there are several literary and poetic devices at play in Longfellow's verses. First, *point of view* (how a story is told) refers to the perspective from which the narrator (here: Longfellow the poet) tells a story. A first person point of view story would be told from the writer's or speaker's perspective, using the pronouns 'I,' 'me,' 'us,' and 'we.' A story told from a second person point of view has the narrator telling her/his story to another character, which could be the audience, and the writer/speaker often uses the pronouns 'you', 'you're' or 'your.' A narrative (story) told from a third person point of view uses the pronouns 'she,' 'he,' 'it' and 'they,' and comes from a removed perspective that comments on both characters and the story's action. First and third person point of view are the most common points of view used by writers/speakers. Longfellow uses two points of view in his poem here. Can you guess both which two points of view Longfellow uses and why he uses those points of view?

Next, note the end-rhyme throughout the poem, which not only preserves and pushes the poem's rhythm but also pulls the reader/speaker into Revere's thoughts as well as into the ride itself. It's as though the reader is making the ride her/himself, hour-by-hour and minute-by-minute, through the Massachusetts countryside as s/he reads! By putting *you* in the saddle, what is the overall message the poet wants *you* to hear? What is/are the '…word(s) that shall echo forevermore!' ?

Then he climbed the tower of the Old North Church,
By the wooden stairs, with stealthy tread,
To the belfry-chamber overhead,
And startled the pigeons from their perch
On the sombre rafters, that round him made
Masses and moving shapes of shade, —
By the trembling ladder, steep and tall,
To the highest window in the wall,
Where he paused to listen and look down
A moment on the roofs of the town,
And the moonlight flowing over all.

Beneath in the churchyard, lay the dead,
In their night-encampment on the hill,
Wrapped in silence so deep and still
That he could hear, like a sentinel's tread,
The watchful night-wind, as it went
Creeping along from tent to tent,
And seeming to whisper, "All is well!"
A moment only he feels the spell
Of the place and the hour, and the secret dread
Of the lonely belfry and the dead;
For suddenly all his thoughts are bent
On a shadowy something far away,
Where the river widens to meet the bay, —
A line of black that bends and floats
On the rising tide, like a bridge of boats.
Meanwhile, impatient to mount and ride,

Booted and spurred, with a heavy stride
On the opposite shore walked Paul Revere.
Now he patted his horse's side,
Now gazed at the landscape far and near,
Then, impetuous, stamped the earth,
And turned and tightened his saddle's girth;
But mostly he watched with eager search
The belfry-tower of the Old North Church,
As it rose above the graves on the hill,
Lonely and spectral and sombre and still.

Notes for **"The Landlord's Tale"** (cont.)

Then Longfellow employs both descriptive and figurative language here to first set the poem's initially dark and impending scene of the British approaching; then next to establish how, from hoof-driven sparks to lamps in the belfry, deliberate and purposeful actions pierce that darkness during the sounding-out of a sentinel's journey wherein "The fate of a nation was riding that night;...." And so, with language, such as "...the spark struck out by that steed, in his flight, Kindled the land into flame with its heat," readers' imaginations are soon both liberated from the creeping yet ominous threat at hand and then quickly placed into the saddled and climactic perspective of 'the ride' itself, coming to rest only as the history books take over at the end of the poem. This visually descriptive and figurative language, for we neither suspect a horse to 'fly' nor a spark's heat to kindle a whole country into 'flames,' appeals to our senses on many levels and is known as *imagery*.

Longfellow adroitly uses *simile* and *metaphor* (both forms of analogy), along with embedded *personification* <u>within</u> similes and metaphors, not only to describe and animate the antagonists, his protagonist, and the countryside but also to create lively visual and sensory images for his readers throughout this poem.

When we compare, or show how things are comparable in order to make clear how two entities resemble each other, we essentially reason by analogy, explaining that <u>this</u> is *analogous* to <u>that</u>. Simpler forms of analogy are the *simile*, where either the word "like" or "as" is used explicitly to compare:

"A phantom ship, with each mast and spar
  Across the moon like a prison bar,...."
and *metaphor*, where the comparison is implicit, **without** using "like" or "as":

"...Is the Mystic, meeting the ocean tides;
  And under the alders, that skirt its edge,...."
  ([*Like*] a skirt, alder trees are 'draped around' the Mystic River's edge.)

Therefore, using metaphors (of which the *simile* is an explicit, direct metaphor) and metaphorical reasoning allow us pathways to compare and communicate the meaning or identity of a subject with another seemingly unrelated subject, whereby our understanding is deepened by their similarities or shared traits.

And lo! as he looks, on the belfry's height
 A glimmer, and then a gleam of light!
He springs to the saddle, the bridle he turns,
But lingers and gazes, till full on his sight
A second lamp in the belfry burns!

A hurry of hoofs in a village street,
A shape in the moonlight, a bulk in the dark,
And beneath, from the pebbles, in passing, a spark
Struck out by a steed flying fearless and fleet:
That was all! And yet, through the gloom and the light,
The fate of a nation was riding that night;
And the spark struck out by that steed, in his flight,
Kindled the land into flame with its heat.
He has left the village and mounted the steep,
And beneath him, tranquil and broad and deep,
Is the Mystic, meeting the ocean tides;
And under the alders, that skirt its edge,
Now soft on the sand, now loud on the ledge,
Is heard the tramp of his steed as he rides.

It was twelve by the village clock,
When he crossed the bridge into Medford town.
He heard the crowing of the cock,
And the barking of the farmer's dog,
And felt the damp of the river's fog,
That rises as the sun goes down.

It was one by the village clock,
When he galloped into Lexington.
He saw the gilded weathercock
Swim in the moonlight as he passed,
And the meeting-house windows, blank and bare,
Gaze at him with a spectral glare,
As if they already stood aghast
At the bloody work they would look upon.

Notes for
"The Landlord's Tale. Paul Revere's Ride." (cont.)

Moreover, Longfellow skillfully uses the literary device called *personification*, which refers to the practice of attaching human traits and characteristics to inanimate objects, events, and animals. Longfellow's use of *personification* in this poem is 'skillful,' for he uses it in conjunction with simile and metaphor in the following passages:

"Beneath, in the churchyard, lay the dead,
 In their night-encampment on the hill,...."
Wrapped in silence so deep and still
That he could hear, like a sentinel's tread,
The watchful night-wind, as it went
Creeping along from tent to tent,
And seeming to whisper, 'All is well!'

(The wind is watchful, creeps and whispers.)
or

"He saw the gilded weathercock
 Swim in the moonlight as he passed.
 And the meeting-house windows, blank and bare,
 Gaze at him with a spectral glare,
 As if they already stood aghast
 At the bloody work they would look upon."

(The gilded weathercock swims;
the windows gaze, stand aghast, and work.)

In fact, *personification* is a form of metaphor, and <u>within</u> the above examples of *personification*, where the wind, weathercock and windows are *personified* with human traits, could you find other examples of simile and metaphor as described earlier?

Through rhyme, rhythm, juxtaposed points-of-view, and by awakening the reader's sensory perceptions through powerful imagery, the poet not only recalls the historical courage of Paul Revere and all those who helped him but also encourages all current and future American patriots to "keep the ride alive."

It was two by the village clock,
When he came to the bridge in Concord town.
He heard the bleating of the flock,
And twitter of birds among the trees,
And felt the breath of the morning breeze
Blowing over the meadows brown.
And one was safe and asleep in his bed
Who at the bridge would be the first to fall,
Who that day would be lying dead,
Pierced by a British musket-ball.

You know the rest. In the books you have read,
How the British Regulars fired and fled, —
How the farmers gave them ball for ball,
From behind each fence and farm-yard wall,
Chasing the red-coats down the lane,
Then crossing the fields to emerge again
Under the trees at the turn of the road,
And only pausing to fire and load.

So through the night rode Paul Revere;
And so through the night went his cry of alarm
To every Middlesex village and farm, —
A cry of defiance and not of fear,
A voice in the darkness, a knock at the door,
And a word that shall echo forevermore!
For, borne on the night-wind of the Past,
Through all our history, to the last,
In the hour of darkness and peril and need,
The people will waken and listen to hear
The hurrying hoof-beats of that steed,
And the midnight message of Paul Revere.

Henry Wadsworth Longfellow

Notes for **"The Theologian's Tale; Elizabeth"**

This poem, "The Theologian's Tale; Elizabeth" (of which we provide only excerpts), is one of the poems included in Henry Wadsworth Longfellow's collection, *Tales of a Wayside Inn*. The idea of the collection was to bring together stories of persons who are staying at an inn and tell tales to each other to pass the time. The most famous of the stories is "The Landlord's Tale. Paul Revere's Ride."

Additionally, one might guess that Longfellow's *Tales of the Wayside Inn* follows somewhat in the tradition of Geoffrey Chaucer's *Canterbury Tales*. One difference is Chaucer's characters were traveling and sharing their stories, while Longfellow's characters shared their stories at the inn where they were staying. The other, perhaps more important difference is that Geoffrey Chaucer wrote in "Middle English," while Henry Wadsworth Longfellow wrote in "Present-day English." You can see just how much has changed over the past 700 years if you compare the language of the two tales!

Reviewing the *Tales of a Wayside Inn* in the *Atlantic Monthly* in 1873, the editor and novelist, William Dean Howells, wrote: "This purely Quaker love-story, in which of course John Estaugh finally 'has freedom' to accept the love of Elizabeth, is perhaps the best in the book. The quaint and homely material is wrought into a texture marvelously delicate; and its colorless fineness clothes a beauty as chaste and soft as the neutral-tinted garments of the fair, meekly bold Quaker maiden. The English hexameter which Mr. Longfellow has so intimately associated with his name, he has never more successfully handled, we think, than in this poem, which recalls *Evangeline* and *The Courtship of Miles Standish* at their best, and yet has a humor and sweetness quite its own, and unmistakably knowable for Longfellow's. But the humor is his quietest, naturally."

"Ships that pass in the night,...."

Tales of a Wayside Inn
The Theologian's Tale; Elizabeth

(excerpts)   ***** = lines omitted

"Ah, how short are the days
            How soon the night overtakes us!
In the old country the twilight is longer;
            but here in the forest
Suddenly comes the dark, with hardly a pause in its coming,
Hardly a moment between the two lights,
            the day and the lamplight;
Yet how grand is the winter!
            How spotless the snow is, and perfect!"

Thus spake Elizabeth Haddon at nightfall
            to Hannah the housemaid,...
"All I have is the Lord's, not mine to give or withhold it;
I but distribute his gifts to the poor,...
We must not grudge, then, to others
Ever the cup of cold water,
            or crumbs that fall from our table."
*****

And he had come as one
            whose coming had long been expected,
Quietly gave him her hand, and said,
            "Thou art welcome, John Estaugh."
And the stranger replied, with staid and quiet behavior,
"Dost thou remember me still, Elizabeth? After so many
Years have passed, it seemeth a wonderful thing
            that I find thee.
Surely the hand of the Lord
            conducted me here to thy threshold...."
*****

Notes for
"The Theologian's Tale; Elizabeth" (cont.)

Henry Wadsworth Longfellow (1807~1882) was a very popular American poet from New England in the 1800s who was a professor of modern languages at Harvard. He wrote mostly long narrative poems such as *The Song of Hiawatha, Evangeline, The Courtship of Miles Standish,* "The Village Blacksmith," and "The Landlord's Tale. Paul Reverse's Ride."

Then Elizabeth said, though still with a certain reluctance,
As if impelled to reveal a secret
        she fain would have guarded:
"I will no longer conceal what is laid upon me to tell thee;
I have received from the Lord
        a charge to love thee, John Estaugh."
*****

"...Thou art going away, across the sea, and I know not
When I shall see thee more;
        but if the Lord hath decreed it,
Thou wilt return again to seek me here and to find me."
And they rode onward in silence,
        and entered the town with the others.
*****

Ships that pass in the night,
        and speak each other in passing,
Only a signal shown and a distant voice in the darkness;
So on the ocean of life we pass and speak one another,
Only a look and a voice, then darkness again and a silence.
Now went on as of old the quiet life of the homestead.
Patient and unrepining Elizabeth labored,....
*****

Then John Estaugh came back o'er the sea
        for the gift that was offered,
Better than houses and lands,
        the gift of a woman's affection.
And on the First-Day that followed,
        he rose in the Silent Assembly,
Holding in his strong hand a hand that trembled a little,
Promising to be kind and true and faithful in all things.
Such were the marriage rites
        of John and Elizabeth Estaugh.
*****

Henry Wadsworth Longfellow

Notes for **"The Raven"**

"The Raven" tells the story of a drowsy and distraught young man in a dark room in December, who is reading in an attempt to forget the death of the lady Lenore of whom he was very fond. After the man first wonders about tapping at his door; then at his window's lattice, a raven enters his room through the window and comes to rest upon the bust of Pallas (the Titan god of warcraft in Greek mythology) above the gentleman's chamber door. The young man questions the bird about its name and the bird says, "Nevermore." Then the man asks the bird if it will leave, just as his "other friends" have left him (such as Lenore), and the bird answers, "Nevermore." Puzzled by the bird and attempting to unravel the riddle of these repeated answers, the young man pulls up a chair and studies the bird wondering why it continues to say "Nevermore." The velvet of the chair reminds the man of Lenore, and so he then asks the bird a series of questions: Can I have nepenthe (a medicine for sorrow)?; Is there balm in Gilead (from the Bible - is there a healing for my people)?, and Will I be able to embrace Lenore in *Aidenn* (Eden -or probably heaven)? And the everpresent bird's answer to all these questions is "Nevermore." Finally, the young man tells the raven to leave and the raven again says "Nevermore."

"Quoth the Raven, 'Nevermore.' "

The Raven

Once upon a midnight dreary,
   while I pondered weak and weary,
Over many a quaint and curious volume of forgotten lore, —
While I nodded, nearly napping,
   suddenly there came a tapping,
As of some one gently rapping,
   rapping at my chamber door.
"'Tis some visitor," I muttered,
   "tapping at my chamber door —
Only this, and nothing more."

Ah, distinctly I remember it was in the bleak December,
And each separate dying ember
   wrought its ghost upon the floor.
Eagerly I wished the morrow;
   - vainly I had sought to borrow
From my books surcease of sorrow —
   sorrow for the lost Lenore —
For the rare and radiant maiden
   whom the angels name Lenore —
Nameless *here* for evermore.

And the silken sad uncertain rustling of each purple curtain
Thrilled me—filled me with fantastic terrors
   never felt before;
So that now, to still the beating of my heart,
   I stood repeating
"'Tis some visitor entreating entrance
   at my chamber door —
Some late visitor entreating entrance at my chamber door;
This it is, and nothing more."

Notes for **"The Raven"** (cont.)

In addition to his spectacular use of internal and end-line rhyme, assonance (vowel rhyming), and alliteration (repetition of consonantal or vocalic sound groups), not to mention the embedded dialog, Poe's generous use of repeating '-ing' word-forms pushes the rhythm of this poem along at a sing-song pace, making the entire verse quite easy to read and remember.

Couching the poem's setting within the darkest time of year, calling both readers' attentions (the young man's as well as the poem's readers) to a "tapping," and positioning the raven atop the bust of Pallas for a dialog that will have no end, Poe brilliantly crafts a war of remembrance from which few people ever really escape. Loss, regret and the past (good or bad) not only inevitably come "tapping" in through the latticework of our memories, just as the raven does in this poem, but also often misleadingly influence ("beguiling") a person's state of consciousness. The word "nevermore" takes on seemingly contradictory meanings of both finality and continuance in this poem, much in the same way one would like to forget or never forget a particular memory. The raven's continued, shadowed presence at the end of the poem reminds the reader that this back-and-forth, internal remembrance dialog never really ends for a person during her/his life. Though many people regard Edgar Allen Poe's works as scary or macabre, his brilliance shines as a writer who not only understood poetic devices but also human psychology quite well.

Are your memories also a sort of shadow that are sometimes difficult to get out from under? What is the cure?

Presently my soul grew stronger;
       hesitating then no longer,
"Sir," said I, "or Madam,
       truly your forgiveness I implore;
But the fact is I was napping,
       and so gently you came rapping,
And so faintly you came tapping,
       tapping at my chamber door,
That I scarce was sure I heard you"—
       here I opened wide the door; —
Darkness there, and nothing more.

Deep into that darkness peering,
       long I stood there wondering, fearing,
Doubting, dreaming dreams
       no mortal ever dared to dream before;
But the silence was unbroken,
       and the darkness gave no token,
And the only word there spoken
       was the whispered word, "Lenore?"
This I whispered, and an echo
       murmured back the word, "Lenore!"
Merely this and nothing more.

Back into the chamber turning,
       all my soul within me burning,
Soon again I heard a tapping somewhat louder than before.
"Surely," said I, "surely
       that is something at my window lattice;
Let me see then, what thereat is,
       and this mystery explore–
Let my heart be still a moment and this mystery explore;—
'Tis the wind and nothing more!"

Notes for **"The Raven"** (cont.)

Edgar Allan Poe (January 19, 1809~October 7, 1849) was an American poet, essayist, critic, and short story writer. As a poet Poe is considered to be part of the Romantic Movement that was flourishing in Europe and especially in England. His poem "The Raven," along with "The Bells," and "Annabel Lee" are some of the best known American poems. Poe is also known for his many tales of mystery, such as *The Cask of the Amontillado* and *The Fall of the House of Usher*, and is credited with having invented the detective story with tales such as *The Mystery of Marie Roget* and *The Murders in the Rue Morgue*.

Moreover, Poe, knowledgeable of Latin, Greek, Spanish, Italian, French and German, was a prolific writer, crafting poems, scores of book reviews, essays, humorous squibs, and stories throughout his short career. The esteemed Poe scholar, Burton Pollin, who died in 2009 at the age of ninety-three, credits Poe with coining, or first using in print, nearly one thousand words. Poe himself said, "I have not suffered a day to pass without writing from a page to three pages." Abraham Lincoln, Fyodor Dostoyevsky, the three great French poets: Baudelaire, Mallarmé and Valéry, George Bernard Shaw, Jules Verne, Herman Melville, and H.P. Lovecraft were all inspired by Edgar Allen Poe, who himself dedicated "The Raven" to Elizabeth Barret Browning, another author whose work you will find in this collection.

Open here I flung the shutter, when,
    with many a flirt and flutter,
In there stepped a stately raven of the saintly days of yore.
Not the least obeisance made he;
    not a minute stopped or stayed he;
But, with mien of lord or lady,
    perched above my chamber door—
Perched upon a bust of Pallas just above my chamber door–
Perched, and sat, and nothing more.

Then this ebony bird beguiling my sad fancy into smiling,
By the grave and stern decorum of the countenance it wore,
"Though thy crest be shorn and shaven,
    thou," I said, "art sure no craven.
Ghastly grim and ancient Raven
    wandering from the nightly shore—
Tell me what thy lordly name is
    on the Night's Plutonian shore!"
Quoth the Raven, "Nevermore."

Much I marvelled this ungainly fowl
    to hear discourse so plainly,
Though its answer little meaning—little relevancy bore;
For we cannot help agreeing that no living human being
Ever yet was blessed with seeing
    bird above his chamber door—
Bird or beast above the sculptured bust
    above his chamber door,—
With such name as "Nevermore."

But the Raven, sitting lonely on the placid bust, spoke only,
That one word, as if his soul
    in that one word he did outpour.
Nothing further then he uttered—
    not a feather then he fluttered —

Notes for **"The Raven"** (cont.)

Finally, Poe, in addition to Washington Irving — who perhaps first introduced the short story form to Americans, was known as another "...father of the American short story." Emphasizing that a short story needed to produce a single effect at its climax, Poe pioneered the short story structure of introduction, exposition, climax, resolution (dénouement), and conclusion to achieve this singular effect in all his short stories. Sir Arthur Conan Doyle, the creator of Sherlock Holmes, called Poe "the supreme original short story writer of all time."

Till I scarcely more than muttered
        "Other friends have flown before—
On the morrow *he* will leave me,
        as my Hopes have flown before."
Then the bird said, "Nevermore."

Startled at the stillness broken by reply so aptly spoken,
"Doubtless," said I, "what it utters
        is its only stock and store,
Caught from some unhappy master
        whom unmerciful disaster
Followed fast and followed faster
        till his songs one burden bore—
Till the dirges of his Hope that melancholy burden bore
Of 'Never — nevermore'."

But the Raven still beguiling all my sad soul into smiling,
Straight I wheeled a cushioned seat
        in front of bird and bust and door;
Then, upon the velvet sinking, I betook myself to linking
Fancy unto fancy, thinking what this ominous bird of yore–
What this grim, ungainly, ghastly, gaunt,
        and ominous bird of yore
Meant in croaking "Nevermore."

This I sat engaged in guessing, but no syllable expressing
To the fowl whose fiery eyes
        now burned into my bosom's core;
This and more I sat divining,
        with my head at ease reclining
On the cushion's velvet lining
        that the lamp-light gloated o'er,
But whose velvet violet lining
        with the lamp-light gloating o'er,
She shall press, ah, nevermore!

WHOSE WORDS THESE ARE

Then, methought, the air grew denser,
  perfumed from an unseen censer
Swung by Seraphim whose foot-falls
  tinkled on the tufted floor.
"Wretch," I cried, "thy God hath lent thee—
  by these angels he has sent thee
Respite—respite and nepenthe
  from thy memories of Lenore!
Quaff, oh quaff this kind nepenthe,
  and forget this lost Lenore!"
Quoth the Raven, "Nevermore."

"Prophet!" said I, "thing of evil!
  — prophet still, if bird or devil! —
Whether tempter sent,
  or whether tempest tossed thee here ashore,
Desolate yet all undaunted, on this desert land enchanted –
On this home by Horror haunted—tell me truly, I implore –
Is there — is there balm in Gilead?
  — tell me — tell me, I implore!"
Quoth the Raven, "Nevermore."

"Prophet!" said I, "thing of evil!
  — prophet still, if bird or devil!
By that Heaven that bends above us —
  by that God we both adore —
Tell this soul with sorrow laden if, within the distant Aidenn,
It shall clasp a sainted maiden
  whom the angels name Lenore —
Clasp a rare and radiant maiden,
  whom the angels name Lenore."
Quoth the Raven, "Nevermore."

WHOSE WORDS THESE ARE

"Be that word our sign of parting, bird or fiend!"
        I shrieked upstarting —
"Get thee back into the tempest
        and the Night's Plutonian shore!
Leave no black plume as a token
        of that lie thy soul hath spoken!
Leave my loneliness unbroken! —
        quit the bust above my door!
Take thy beak from out my heart,
        and take thy form from off my door!"
Quoth the Raven, "Nevermore."

And the Raven, never flitting, still is sitting, *still* is sitting
On the pallid bust of Pallas just above my chamber door;
And his eyes have all the seeming
        of a demon's that is dreaming,
And the lamp-light o'er him streaming
        throws his shadow on the floor;
And my soul from out that shadow
        that lies floating on the floor
Shall be lifted — nevermore!

Edgar Allen Poe

Notes for **"To Helen"**

Though this poem was originally published in 1831, "To Helen" went through several revisions and is thought to be a tribute to Poe's good friend Robert Stanard's mother Jane Stith Stanard, a woman who encouraged Edgar Allen Poe (then fourteen years old) to write poetry, and who had recently passed away. We do not know exactly why Poe uses the name "Helen;" however, the renaming is generally attributed to the poet's transcendent love and respect for Ms. Stanard, which he signifies by elevating this woman's inner and outer beauty first to the mythical beauty of Helen of Troy, a Grecian woman born in Sparta.

Reputedly the most beautiful woman in the world, Helen was kidnapped by the Trojan prince Paris around 1200 BCE and taken to Troy. The ten-year Trojan War of Homer's *Iliad* was the conflict whereby Greeks attacked Troy to bring her back. "Nicean barks" may refer to victorious ships (Nike was the winged god of victory; "barks" are ships; and the Greeks returned home from Troy victorious). Hence, the first stanza suggests Ms. Stanard (now "Helen") would be both the type of beauty both worth fighting for and the pursuit of a seafaring wanderer returning to his native shores. Moreover, the nautical imagery here may be intended to remind the reader that the playwright Christopher Marlowe, in his Elizabethan tragedy *Doctor Faustus* (first performed sometime between 1588 and Marlowe's death in 1593), referred to Helen of Troy's countenance as "the face that launched a thousand ships."

The second stanza continues with elevated references to mythical beauty: her "hyacinth hair" (the fragrant hyacinth flower being "the gem of the ancients"); her "classic face," yet it is her "Naiad airs" (songs/breezes from the water nymphs of Nysa — of Greek mythical lore) that bring this writer "home." Critics suggest that Poe, at such a young age, felt more comfortable at the Stanard's homestead than other environments, being encouraged to write and to continue with learning the classics.

**"…the glory that was Greece,
And the grandeur that was Rome."**

To Helen

Helen, thy beauty is to me
  Like those Nicéan barks of yore,
That gently, o'er a perfumed sea,
  The weary, way-worn wanderer bore
  To his own native shore.

On desperate seas long wont to roam,
  Thy hyacinth hair, thy classic face,
Thy Naiad airs have brought me home
  To the glory that was Greece,
  And the grandeur that was Rome.

Lo! in yon brilliant window-niche
  How statue-like I see thee stand,
The agate lamp within thy hand!
  Ah, Psyche, from the regions which
  Are Holy-Land!

Edgar Allen Poe

Notes for **"To Helen"** (cont.)

Hence, the full celebration at the end of second stanza: "To the glory that was Greece, / And the grandeur that was Rome." These two lines were originally written in Poe's 1831 version as "To the beauty of fair Greece/And the grandeur of old Rome." Poe's revision created two memorable lines that sum up classical Western civilization.

Finally, the third stanza's mythical allusion is to Psyche, a beautiful princess in both Greek and Roman mythology dear to Eros (Cupid), whose previously unknown identity is finally discovered by Psyche's "agate lamp" raised in the darkened room where they usually met. After some tribulations, Eros convinces Zeus to make Psyche immortal, and they marry. Here too Poe thus immortalizes and conflates Ms. Stanard's (now "Helen's") outer beauty of her standing silhouette ("statue-like") in the window with her inner beauty — her "psyche," bearing her 'lamp of learning' or beacon of classical knowledge as revealed to Poe. Thus, the regions where this "Helen" dwells are to the poet a "Holy-Land."

Edgar Allan Poe (January 19, 1809~October 7, 1849) was an American poet and short story writer. As a poet he is considered as part of the Romantic Movement that was flourishing in Europe and especially in England. His poem "The Raven," along with "The Bells," and "Annabel Lee" are some of the best known American poems. In addition to his poetry, Poe is known for his tales of mystery such as *The Cask of Amontillado* and *The Fall of the House of Usher.* He is also credited with having invented the detective story with tales such as *The Mystery of Marie Roget* and *The Murders in the Rue Morgue.*

Notes for **"Maud Muller"**

This poem, written in fifty-five rhymed couplets (as presented here where limited space required that some couplets be merged, some lines deleted and a summary be added), tells of a beautiful country maid who meets a wealthy judge. Each is attracted to the other. In the deleted lines the years pass, the judge marries a woman who is after his money, and the maid marries an uneducated farmer. As their lives go on, each remembers that day of meeting and wonders what might have been if only one of them had taken some action.

The poem's lines "what might have been" speaks to a common situation for many persons who have had chance encounters and have not followed-up on those encounters. Is the poet suggesting that our "stations" in life can sometimes become prisons of sorts when we neither exercise good 'judgement' of favorable chances presented nor take advantage of opportunities that come our way? Compare the theme of this poem with Brutus' speech from *Julius Caesar* Act 4; Scene 3 in this collection.

**" For of all sad words of tongue or pen,
The saddest are these: 'It might have been!' "**

Maud Muller

***** = omitted lines

Maud Muller, on a summer's day,
Raked the meadows sweet with hay.
Beneath her torn hat glowed the wealth
Of simple beauty and rustic health.
Singing, she wrought, and her merry glee
The mock-bird echoed from his tree.
But, when she glanced to the far-off town,
White from its hill-slope looking down,
*****

A wish, that she hardly dared to own,
For something better than she had known.

The Judge rode slowly down the lane,
Smoothing his horse's chestnut mane.
He drew his bridle in the shade
Of the apple-trees, to greet the maid,
And ask a draught from the spring that flowed
Through the meadow across the road.

She stooped where the cool spring bubbled up,
And filled for him her small tin cup,
And blushed as she gave it, looking down
On her feet so bare, and her tattered gown.
"Thanks!" said the Judge, "a sweeter draught
From a fairer hand was never quaffed."
He spoke of the grass and flowers and trees,
Of the singing birds and the humming bees;
***** (*The Judge then rides on*)
Maud Muller looked and sighed: "Ah, me!
That I the Judge's bride might be!..."

Notes for **"Maud Muller"** (cont.)

John Greenleaf Whittier (1807~1892) was an American poet and editor. He wrote of religion, nature and New England life, became the most popular rural New England poet in the nineteenth century, and is said to have been the poet of the country folk. His most famous poems are "Barbara Fritchie" (1863), "Maud Muller" (1854), "The Barefoot Boy" (1865), and "Snowbound" (1866).

The Judge looked back as he climbed the hill,
And saw Maud Muller standing still.
*****

"Would she were mine, and I to-day,
Like her, a harvester of hay:..."
***** (*in the poem, the years pass*)-------
Oft when the wine in his glass was red,
He longed for the wayside well instead;
And closed his eyes on his garnished rooms,
To dream of meadows and clover-blooms.
  *****

And oft, when the summer sun shone hot
On the new-mown hay in the meadow lot,
And she heard the little spring brook fall
Over the roadside, through the wall,

In the shade of the apple-tree again
She saw a rider draw his rein,
And, gazing down with timid grace,
She felt his pleased eyes read her face.
Sometimes her narrow kitchen walls
Stretched away into stately halls;
*****

A manly form at her side she saw,
And joy was duty and love was law.
Then she took up her burden of life again,
Saying only, "It might have been."

Alas for maiden, alas for Judge,
For rich repiner and household drudge!
God pity them both! and pity us all,
Who vainly the dreams of youth recall;
For of all sad words of tongue or pen,
The saddest are these: "It might have been!"

John Greenleaf Whittier

Notes for **"The Rubaiyat of Omar Khayyam"**

"The Rubáiyát of Omar Khayyám" is the title that Edward FitzGerald gave to his translation of a personal selection, in no particular sequence, from about a thousand poems that were originally written in Persian in 1120 by the Persian poet, mathematician and astronomer Omar Khayyám (1048~1131). FitzGerald himself pointed out that his translation was not literal. Many of the four line verses are altered, and others cannot be traced to any one of Khayyam's quatrains. The first edition of 'the Rubaiyat' was published in 1859; the last, with 101 quatrains, was published in 1889.

As these quatrains are in Roman numbers, let us look at how to decipher and convert Roman numbers to Arabic numbers:

I=1; II=2; III=3; IV=4; V=5;
VI=6; VII=7; VIII=8; IX=9, and X=10.

So, X+II (XII here) = the 12th quatrain (or quatrain number 12), and XIII= the 13th quatrain. XX would then equal 20 (here XXIV=24), and XXX=30. The Roman L=50, so can you figure out how XLIX equals 49? Here the Roman LIV=54; LXIII would equal 63, and LXXI = 71. If the Roman numeral C = 100, then what would be the Arabic equivalent of the Roman numeral XCIX? Furthermore, the Roman numeral D = 500, and M = 1000. The Arabic number 900 in Roman numerology would then be CM. Google the Roman to Arabic number conversions and learn the rules @

periodni.com/roman_numerals_converter.html

and have some fun!

This poem both reflects in most part FitzGerald's *carpe diem* (seize the day), both a "live for today" philosophy and his meditations on the transience of all things.

"A Book of Verses Underneath the Bough
A Jug of wine, a Loaf of Bread, – and Thou…."

"Ah, take the Cash, and let the Credit go,…."

"The Moving Finger writes; and, having writ,
Moves on:…."

The Rubaiyat of Omar Khayyam
(Excerpts from 5th Edition 1889)

I

Wake! For the Sun, who scatter'd into flight
The Stars before him from the Field of Night,
Drives Night along with them from Heav'n, and strikes
The Sultan's Turret with a Shaft of Light.

XII

A Book of Verses underneath the Bough,
A Jug of Wine, a Loaf of Bread -- and Thou
Beside me singing in the Wilderness -
Oh, Wilderness were Paradise enow!

XIII

Some for the Glories of This World; and some
Sigh for the Prophet's Paradise to come;
Ah, take the Cash, and let the Credit go,
Nor heed the rumble of a distant Drum!

XXIV

Ah, make the most of what we yet may spend,
Before we too into the Dust descend;
Dust into Dust, and under Dust to lie
Sans Wine, sans Song, sans Singer, and — sans End!

Notes for **"The Rubaiyat of Omar Khayyam"**
(cont.)

Edward Marlborough FitzGerald (March 31, 1809~June 14, 1883) was an English writer born in Suffolk, England in 1809 to one of the wealthiest families in all of Britain. He spent some of his early years with his parents in France and then returned to England to attend Trinity College, Cambridge. After college he moved back to Suffolk and lived quietly in the country, not leaving his home for more than a week or two, usually to visit his friends, the poet Alfred Lord Tennyson and the novelist William Makepeace Thackeray. In 1853 he studied Persian literature at Oxford. He married Lucy Barton on November 4, 1856, but they separated only a few months later. FitzGerald is best known for the first and most famous English translation of "The Rubáiyát of Omar Khayyam."

LIV

Waste not your Hour, nor in the vain pursuit
Of This and That endeavour and dispute;
Better be jocund with the fruitful Grape
Than sadden after none, or bitter, Fruit.

LXIII

Oh, threats of Hell and Hopes of Paradise!
One thing at least is certain — This Life flies;
One thing is certain and the rest is Lies;
The Flower that once has blown for ever dies.

LXXI

The Moving Finger writes; and, having writ,
Moves on: nor all your Piety nor Wit
Shall lure it back to cancel half a Line,
Nor all your Tears wash out a Word of it.

Edward FitzGerald

Notes for **"Charge of the Light Brigade"**

This poem was written to commemorate a British cavalry brigade that, due to a miscommunication in orders, was sent to charge a formidable Russian artillery battery on October 25, 1854 at Balaclava during the Crimean War. The brigade was decimated.

Alfred Lord Tennyson (1809~1892) was Poet Laureate of England from 1850 to 1892. The duties of the Poet Laureate are to write poems in honor of the sovereign's birthday and poems to commemorate important state events.

Tennyson published this poem on December 2, 1854, six weeks after the battle.

The famous lines in this poem are:

> **"Theirs not to make reply,**
> **Theirs not to reason why,**
> **Theirs but to do and die.**
> **Into the valley of Death**
> **Rode the six hundred."**

The lines "Into the valley of death" are no doubt intended to recall the words of the famous 23rd Psalm from the Bible (also in this collection): "Though I walk through the valley of the shadow of death, I will fear no evil."

Incidentally, James Thomas Brudenell, the British Army Major General who led the Light Brigade at the Battle of Balaclava against the Russians, was also the seventh Earl of Cardigan. The Cardigan sweater or jacket derives its name from this collarless upper-garment worn by Lord Cardigan during the early-to-mid nineteenth century. Lord Cardigan was the first-in and first-out of the attack on the Russian guns. He emerged, as opposed to the other 600 soldiers, unscathed.

ALFRED LORD TENNYSON

**"Theirs not to reason why,
Theirs but to do and die."**

The Charge of the Light Brigade

I

Half a league, half a league,
Half a league onward,
All in the valley of Death
　　Rode the six hundred.
"Forward, the Light Brigade!
Charge for the guns!" he said.
Into the valley of Death
　　Rode the six hundred.

II

"Forward, the Light Brigade!"
Was there a man dismayed?
Not though the soldier knew
　　Someone had blundered.
　　Theirs not to make reply,
　　Theirs not to reason why,
　　Theirs but to do and die.
　　Into the valley of Death
　　Rode the six hundred.

III

Cannon to right of them,
Cannon to left of them,
Cannon in front of them
　　Volleyed and thundered;
Stormed at with shot and shell,
Boldly they rode and well,
Into the jaws of Death,
Into the mouth of hell
　　Rode the six hundred.

Notes for **"Charge of the Light Brigade** (cont.)

To imitate the rhythm of horses charging, Tennyson made use in this poem of the *dactylic* measure: long syllable followed by two short syllables, as in

DUM da da — DUM da da

Poets also use what is called *anapest* measure (two short syllables followed by a long syllable, as in *da da Dum. da da Dum*) to represent the rhythm of a galloping horse.

A contemporary of Tennyson, Robert Browning, used the anapest measure in his poem "How They Brought the Good News from Ghent to Aix," describing an imaginary historical event with riders galloping tough the night to convey a message. Longfellow too used the anapest in a similar poem about a true event, "The Landlord's Tale. Paul Revere's Ride."

Alfred Lord Tennyson (1809~1892), the Poet Laureate of England during the reign of Queen Victoria (The Victorian Age: 1837-1901), wrote many famous poems; among them "The Charge of the Light Brigade" and "Ulysses."

IV

Flashed all their sabres bare,
Flashed as they turned in air
Sabring the gunners there,
Charging an army, while
 All the world wondered.
Plunged in the battery-smoke
Right through the line they broke;
Cossack and Russian
Reeled from the sabre stroke
 Shattered and sundered.
Then they rode back, but not
 Not the six hundred.

V

Cannon to right of them,
Cannon to left of them,
Cannon behind them
 Volleyed and thundered;
Stormed at with shot and shell,
While horse and hero fell.
They that had fought so well
Came through the jaws of Death,
Back from the mouth of hell,
All that was left of them,
 Left of six hundred.

VI

When can their glory fade?
O the wild charge they made!
 All the world wondered.
Honour the charge they made!
Honour the Light Brigade,
 Noble six hundred!

Alfred Lord Tennyson

Notes for **"Flower in the Crannied Wall"**

The poet contemplates that the smallest thing in nature, one that a person might find anywhere, is part of the whole of creation. He says that if we could understand it--see how it worked, see how it was put together - we would know about man and God because the whole of the universe can be understood from an examination of its parts. Here the final "is," a singular verb aligned with the singular subject "what," serves a more *plural* purpose: the inclusivity of all things great and small – "...all in all,...."

Starting with the word "Flower," Tennyson generously uses the poetic device of **alliteration** (the occurrence of the same letter or sound at the beginning of adjacent or closely connected words), contrasting the vowel 'a' with 'o' and allowing the consonants 'l' and 'h' to *stretch* both of these vowels in certain words and phrases. Through additional rhyming of vowel sounds — known as **assonance** — Tennyson cleverly uses both poetic devices to tie together the sublime and the divine. Say aloud "crannied," "hand," "understand" and "man;" then all the words containing the vowel 'o.' Feel how the words grow and recede, and again grow and recede accordingly. Here in this seemingly simple and short poem is the "pulse of creation and the universe," what a root is to a flower, and what God is to man — parts unto their whole; a whole unto its parts. Sometimes the simplest things produce profound revelations, and here is evidence of Tennyson's verse mastery in that regard.

One might compare this poem to William Blake's opening lines from "Auguries of Innocence" (also in this collection):

"To see a World in a Grain of Sand...."

Alfred Lord Tennyson (1809~1892) became the Poet Laureate of England during the reign of Queen Victoria (The Victorian Age: 1837-1901).

"Flower in the crannied wall,…."

Flower in the Crannied Wall

Flower in the crannied wall,
I pluck you out of the crannies,
I hold you here, root and all, in my hand,
Little flower - but if I could understand
What you are, root and all, and all in all,
I should know what God and man is.

Alfred Lord Tennyson

Notes for **"The Eagle"**

Eagles, like hawks and falcons, are in the class called "raptors," that is, birds who prey on other birds and small and medium sized animals.

This scene describes an eagle perched on a mountain top near the sea. The eagle watches and then "falls," meaning he dives upon his prey "like a thunderbolt."

This very famous short poem by Tennyson is often the first poem taught to students not familiar with poetry.

It not only shows how rhyme works, but also points out:

1. **_alliteration_** (sharp rough words such as clasps, crag, crooked, close, crawls evoke toughness) and

2. **_personification_** (The Eagle is a "he," and said to have "hands," not claws; the "wrinkled sea," waves, as observed from far above, "crawls" as if the sea were a person).

Also, the poet does not write that the eagle is up high, but says he is "close to the sun" and "ringed with the azure world." Finally, the word _eagle_ does not appear in the poem, so the title really is part of the poem.

The idea is to show that poetry can often give a better feeling about a subject (here an eagle) than a dictionary definition.

Alfred Lord Tennyson (1809~1892), the Poet Laureate of England during the reign of Queen Victoria (The Victorian Age: 1837-1901), wrote many famous poems; among them "The Charge of the Light Brigade" and "Ulysses."

"...like a thunderbolt he falls."

The Eagle

He clasps the crag with crooked hands;
Close to the sun in lonely lands,
Ring'd with the azure world, he stands.

The wrinkled sea beneath him crawls;
He watches from his mountain walls,
And like a thunderbolt he falls.

Alfred Lord Tennyson

Notes for **"The Passing of Arthur"**

In addition to his many short poems, such as "The Charge of the Light Brigade," during the years 1859~1885, Alfred Lord Tennyson wrote a series of narrative poems (narrative poems tell a story) in ten books which collectively are called *The Idylls of the King* based on the legend of King Arthur and the Round Table.

The last of these ten books is called *The Passing of Arthur*. In this book, Arthur, accompanied by the last surviving knight Sir Bedivere, went to the ocean shore and asked the knight to throw Arthur's sword "Excalibur" into the sea. When Sir Bedivere did so, a hand reached up out of the sea, seized the sword, brandished it three times, and took it down under the waves. Then a dusky barge approached with three queens crowned with gold. King Arthur asked Sir Bedivere to help him into the barge where the three queens took his hands. Sir Bedivere then called to Arthur as the barge departed, "Ah! my Lord Arthur, whither shall I go?" and this is the way the poem concludes.

One of the two most notable lines in this selection: "The old order changeth, yielding place to new,..." seems to be echoed in Bob Dylan's "The Times They Are A-Changin'," written some one hundred years later in 1964 and cited in this collection.

Alfred Lord Tennyson (1809~1892) was the Poet Laureate of England during the reign of Queen Victoria (The Victorian Age: 1837~1901).

**"The old order changeth,
yielding place to new,…."**

**"More things are wrought by prayer
Than this world dreams of."**

The Passing of Arthur

Then loudly cried the bold Sir Bedivere:
"Ah! my Lord Arthur, whither shall I go?
Where shall I hide my forehead and my eyes?
For now I see the true old times are dead,
When every morning brought a noble chance,
And every chance brought out a noble knight.
Such times have been not since the light that led
The holy Elders with the gift of myrrh.
But now the whole Round Table is dissolved
Which was an image of the mighty world,
And I, the last, go forth companionless,
And the days darken round me, and the years,
Among new men, strange faces, other minds."

And slowly answer'd Arthur from the barge:
"The old order changeth, yielding place to new,
And God fulfils himself in many ways,
Lest one good custom should corrupt the world.
Comfort thyself: what comfort is in me?
I have lived my life, and that which I have done
May He within himself make pure! but thou,
If thou shouldst never see my face again,
Pray for my soul. More things are wrought by prayer
Than this world dreams of. Wherefore, let thy voice
Rise like a fountain for me night and day.
For what are men better than sheep or goats
That nourish a blind life within the brain,
If, knowing God, they lift not hands of prayer
Both for themselves and those who call them friend?"
                                    Alfred Lord Tennyson

Notes for **"Ulysses"**

Written in 1842, "Ulysses" is a 70-line poem by Alfred Lord Tennyson about the great Greek warrior of that name who returned to his home after fighting against the Trojans for ten years alongside his fellow warrior Achilles. Homer's poem "The Odyssey" ends after Ulysses (in Greek called Odysseus) comes home to Ithaca (where he is King), to his wife Penelope, who has waited many years for his return, and to his son, Telemachus.

In this poem Tennyson imagines that Ulysses is restless for more action before he dies: ("something ere the end …may yet be done"). In the first five lines of the poem Ulysses contemplates his present situation. He is king, but his people do not really know him. In the next twelve lines he thinks about his travels, how he was "always roaming" and reflects on his experiences. "How dull it is," he says, to end these adventures and to let his life "rust" rather than "shine…."

Ulysses then decides to hand over the rule of the land to his son, Telemachus, sure that "by slow prudence" Telemachus, as king, will "make mild /A rugged people, and thro' soft degrees / Subdue them to the useful and the good."

Ulysses sees his ship at the shore with sails billowing and determines to gather his men: ("Come my friends") to set off on another adventure, ("Push off" from shore) and get ready to row ("sitting well in order smite").

Because this poem is set in the evening ("The lights begin to twinkle from the rocks: / The long day wanes: the slow moon climbs: the deep"), some critics suggest Tennyson has Ulysses thinking not of a journey but of his own death, which ironically is also yet another unknown 'passage' for us all.

" 'Tis not too late to seek a newer world. "

"To strive, to seek, to find, and not to yield."

Ulysses

It little profits that an idle king,
By this still hearth, among these barren crags,
Match'd with an aged wife, I mete and dole
Unequal laws unto a savage race,
That hoard, and sleep, and feed, and know not me.
I cannot rest from travel: I will drink
Life to the lees: All times I have enjoy'd
Greatly, have suffer'd greatly, both with those
That loved me, and alone, on shore, and when
Thro' scudding drifts the rainy Hyades
Vext the dim sea: I am become a name;
For always roaming with a hungry heart
Much have I seen and known; cities of men
And manners, climates, councils, governments,
Myself not least, but honour'd of them all;
And drunk delight of battle with my peers,
Far on the ringing plains of windy Troy.
I am a part of all that I have met;
Yet all experience is an arch wherethro'
Gleams that untravell'd world whose margin fades
For ever and forever when I move.
How dull it is to pause, to make an end,
To rust unburnish'd, not to shine in use!
As tho' to breathe were life! Life piled on life
Were all too little, and of one to me
Little remains: but every hour is saved
From that eternal silence, something more,
A bringer of new things; and vile it were
For some three suns to store and hoard myself,
And this gray spirit yearning in desire
To follow knowledge like a sinking star,
Beyond the utmost bound of human thought.

Notes for **"Ulysses"** (cont.)

This poem is a dramatic monologue written in unrhymed iambic pentameter, that is, iambic measure (short syllable - long syllable, *da DUM)* and five measures to a line. For a poem with rhymed iambic pentameter, see Robert Browning's "My Last Duchess" in this collection. Browning, like Tennyson, wrote dramatic monologues during the Victorian Era.

The memorable lines in this poem are: "'Tis not too late to seek a newer world" and "To strive, to seek, to find, and not to yield." In 1941, the great, outdoor-education organization Outward Bound adopted and modified this latter memorable line to become its operational motto: 'To serve, to strive, and not to yield.'

Alfred Lord Tennyson (1809~1892) became the Poet Laureate of England during the reign of Queen Victoria (The Victorian Age 1837-1901).

This is my son, mine own Telemachus,
To whom I leave the sceptre and the isle,—
Well-loved of me, discerning to fulfil
This labour, by slow prudence to make mild
A rugged people, and thro' soft degrees
Subdue them to the useful and the good.
Most blameless is he, centred in the sphere
Of common duties, decent not to fail
In offices of tenderness, and pay
Meet adoration to my household gods,
When I am gone. He works his work, I mine.

There lies the port; the vessel puffs her sail:
There gloom the dark, broad seas. My mariners,
Souls that have toil'd, and wrought, and thought with me
That ever with a frolic welcome took
The thunder and the sunshine, and opposed
Free hearts, free foreheads — you and I are old;
Old age hath yet his honour and his toil;
Death closes all: but something ere the end,
Some work of noble note, may yet be done,
Not unbecoming men that strove with Gods.
The lights begin to twinkle from the rocks:
The long day wanes: the slow moon climbs: the deep
Moans round with many voices. Come, my friends,
'Tis not too late to seek a newer world.
Push off, and sitting well in order smite
The sounding furrows; for my purpose holds
To sail beyond the sunset, and the baths
Of all the western stars, until I die.
It may be that the gulfs will wash us down:
It may be we shall touch the Happy Isles,
And see the great Achilles, whom we knew.
Tho' much is taken, much abides; and tho'
We are not now that strength which in old days
Moved earth and heaven, that which we are, we are;
One equal temper of heroic hearts,
Made weak by time and fate, but strong in will
To strive, to seek, to find, and not to yield.

Alfred Lord Tennyson

Notes for **"My Last Duchess"**

This poem is one of Robert Browning's dramatic monologues. Here the speaker, obviously a Duke who intends to marry the Count's daughter, is giving an emissary from the Count a tour of his castle.

During the tour he shows a picture of his "last Duchess" painted by the painter Fra Pandolf to the Count's emissary. The Duke describes the painting and the personality of the last Duchess, who apparently, in her flirtatious naiveté, found joy in everything and everyone, treating her benefactor (the Duke) the same as she treated everyone. Disgusted, the Duke then "…gave commands."

Concluding, the Duke says that he is not interested in what will be a large dowry but rather in the Count's fair daughter for marriage. Finally, the Duke points out a work cast in bronze for him by a famous artist.

What do you think happened to the Duke's last Duchess? Do you find any measure of jealousy or conceit in the Duke's character? What do you think happened after the Duke "gave commands"? Would you fear for the Count's fair daughter?

If you were the emissary, when you returned to the Count, what report about the Duke would you give to the Count?

This poem is written in iambic pentameter with rhymed couplets, but Browning does not end sentences at the end of a line, so the rhyme is hardly noticed. The technical term for continuation of a sentence beyond the end of a poetic line is "enjambment."

**"I gave commands;
Then all smiles stopped…"**

My Last Duchess

That's my last Duchess painted on the wall,
Looking as if she were alive. I call
That piece a wonder, now; Fra Pandolf's hands
Worked busily a day, and there she stands.
Will't please you sit and look at her? I said
"Fra Pandolf" by design, for never read
Strangers like you that pictured countenance,
The depth and passion of its earnest glance,
But to myself they turned (since none puts by
The curtain I have drawn for you, but I)
And seemed as they would ask me, if they durst,
How such a glance came there; so, not the first
Are you to turn and ask thus. Sir, 'twas not
Her husband's presence only, called that spot
Of joy into the Duchess' cheek; perhaps
Fra Pandolf chanced to say, "Her mantle laps
Over my lady's wrist too much," or "Paint
Must never hope to reproduce the faint
Half-flush that dies along her throat." Such stuff
Was courtesy, she thought, and cause enough
For calling up that spot of joy. She had
A heart — how shall I say? — too soon made glad,
Too easily impressed; she liked whate'er
She looked on, and her looks went everywhere.
Sir, 'twas all one! My favour at her breast,
The dropping of the daylight in the West,

Notes for **"My Last Duchess"** (cont.)

Robert Browning (1812~1889) was a famous English poet who wrote dramatic verse. Although he wrote many poems, he was unable to make much money from his poetry until 1869 when he published *The Ring and the Book*, a long poem about an Italian murder case in the late 17th century.

The bough of cherries some officious fool
Broke in the orchard for her, the white mule
She rode with round the terrace — all and each
Would draw from her alike the approving speech,
Or blush, at least. She thanked men — good!
    but thanked
Somehow — I know not how — as if she ranked
My gift of a nine-hundred-years-old name
With anybody's gift. Who'd stoop to blame
This sort of trifling? Even had you skill
In speech — which I have not — to make your will
Quite clear to such an one, and say, "Just this
Or that in you disgusts me; here you miss,
Or there exceed the mark" — and if she let
Herself be lessoned so, nor plainly set
Her wits to yours, forsooth, and made excuse —
E'en then would be some stooping; and I choose
Never to stoop. Oh, sir, she smiled, no doubt,
Whene'er I passed her; but who passed without
Much the same smile? This grew; I gave commands;
Then all smiles stopped together. There she stands
As if alive. Will't please you rise? We'll meet
The company below, then. I repeat,
The Count your master's known munificence
Is ample warrant that no just pretense
Of mine for dowry will be disallowed;
Though his fair daughter's self, as I avowed
At starting, is my object. Nay, we'll go
Together down, sir. Notice Neptune, though,
Taming a sea-horse, thought a rarity,
Which Claus of Innsbruck cast in bronze for me!

Robert Browning

Notes for **"Pippa Passes"**

This famous fragment of a poem appears in the middle of Part I of Robert Browning's play *Pippa Passes*.

The play was Browning's first important work and tells of Pippa, a little Italian girl, who passes by and her singing influences the lives of four groups of people.

The stage direction preceding this fragment is "*From without is heard the voice of* PIPPA *singing* —." The direction immediately following is "[PIPPA passes]." Because of this stage direction, the poem is often called *Pippa Passes* or *Pippa's Song*.

The line "God's in His heaven – All's right with the world" is often used by those wish to express an optimistic view of life. Note the morning moment of perfection.

Robert Browning (1812~1889), was an English poet who wrote dramatic verse. Browning wrote many other much more serious and long poems, most notable, *The Ring and the Book*, "The Pied Piper of Hamelin" and the dramatic monologues "My Last Duchess" and "Fra Lippo Lippi." He was married to the poet Elizabeth Barrett Browning.

**"God's in His heaven –
All's right with the world."**

Pippa Passes

The year's at the spring
And day's at the morn
Morning's at seven;
The hillside's dew pearled;
The Lark's on the wing;
The snail's on the thorn;
God's in His heaven –
All's right with the world.

Robert Browning

Notes for **"I Hear America Singing"**

This poem, celebrating the average American worker who does his task and so contributes to the greatness of America, was published in the 1867 edition of Whitman's collection of poems *Leaves of Grass* (An earlier version was published in the 1860 edition).

(The theme of each person and thing expressing its own individuality was echoed by Gerard Manley Hopkins in the sonnet "Kingfishers Catch Fire" written in 1877. Hopkins, an admirer of Whitman, saw, however, that each individual and thing, by being itself, reflected not the greatness of his country, England, but rather the glory of God and the universe.)

Walt Whitman (1819~1892) was a newspaper editor, a writer and a poet who developed a new free verse approach to poetry which disregarded rhyme and meter. For Whitman the poetic unit was the line and parallelism was the rhythmic device. Whitman published his first volume of poetry *Leaves of Grass* in July, 1855. In the first and longest of poems in the volume "Song of Myself," the author writes that he represents all of humankind because he can identify with every person, the slave, the fireman, the artilleryman, and others. One really needs to read Whitman's long poems to appreciate his style, but here are two short samples from *Leaves of Grass*:

"Not I, nor anyone else can travel that road for you.
　You must travel it by yourself.
　It is not far. It is within reach.
　Perhaps you have been on it since you were born,
　and did not know.
　Perhaps it is everywhere - on water and land."
　　　　　　　********

"Have you reckon'd a thousand acres much?
　have you reckon'd the earth much?
　Have you practis'd so long to learn to read?
　Have you felt so proud to get at the meaning of poems?"

"I hear America singing,...."

I Hear America Singing

I hear America singing, the varied carols I hear,
Those of mechanics, each one singing his
   as it should be blithe and strong,
The carpenter singing his
   as he measures his plank or beam,
The mason singing his as he makes ready for work,
   or leaves off work,
The boatman singing what belongs to him in his boat,
   the deckhand singing on the steamboat deck,
The shoemaker singing as he sits on his bench,
   the hatter singing as he stands,
The wood-cutter's song, the ploughboy's on his way in
   the morning, or at noon intermission or at sundown,
The delicious singing of the mother, or of the young wife
   at work, or of the girl sewing or washing,
Each singing what belongs to him or her
   and to none else,
The day what belongs to the day—at night the party
   of young fellows, robust, friendly,
Singing with open mouths their strong melodious songs.

Walt Whitman

Notes for **"O Captain!, My Captain!"**

Walt Whitman wrote two significant poems about the death of President Lincoln. "When Lilacs Last in the Dooryard Bloom'd" is a long poem in Whitman's unique style; the other poem, "O Captain!, My Captain!" was written in traditional rhyme.

"My Captain" refers to Abraham Lincoln. The "ship" refers to the "ship of state," the United States. In the movie *Dead Poets Society* (1989), Robin Williams, who played a private boys' school teacher (Mr. Keating), references "Uncle Walt" [Whitman] throughout classroom scenes and is in turn referred to as "O Captain! My Captain!" by his students as he leaves the classroom and school.

Walt Whitman (1819~1892), born on Long Island, N.Y. was a newspaper editor, a writer and a poet, who developed a new free verse approach to poetry which disregarded rhyme and meter. For Whitman the poetic unit was the line of verse, and parallelism was the rhythmic device.

At age thirty-four, Whitman published his first volume of poetry *Leaves of Grass* in July, 1855. He sent a copy to Ralph Waldo Emerson who responded, "I am not blind to the worth of the wonderful gift of 'Leaves of Grass.' I find it the most extraordinary piece of wit and wisdom that America has yet contributed...I greet you at the beginning of a great career which yet must have had a long foreground somewhere for such a start." Whitman published the letter in the book's next edition in 1856. Emerson's approval set in motion Whitman's career as a poet.

The Yale critic, Harold Bloom, said that "Whitman, along with Emily Dickinson, is one of the two great American poet-originals."

Whitman had a tremendous effect on all poets after him. As the Nobel laureate novelist Ernest Hemingway said, "All modern American literature comes from one book by Mark Twain called *Huckleberry Finn*," so one might also say that all American poetry after the Civil War was very much influenced by Walt Whitman.

"O Captain! my Captain!"

O Captain! My Captain!

O Captain! my Captain! our fearful trip is done,
The ship has weather'd every rack, the prize we sought is won,
The port is near, the bells I hear, the people all exulting,
While follow eyes the steady keel, the vessel grim and daring;

But O heart! heart! heart!
O the bleeding drops of red,
Where on the deck my Captain lies,
Fallen cold and dead.

O Captain! my Captain! rise up and hear the bells;
Rise up — for you the flag is flung — for you the bugle trills,
For you bouquets and ribbon'd wreaths — for you the shores
a-crowding,
For you they call, the swaying mass, their eager faces turning;

Here Captain! dear father!
The arm beneath your head!
It is some dream that on the deck,
You've fallen cold and dead.

My Captain does not answer, his lips are pale and still,
My father does not feel my arm, he has no pulse nor will,
The ship is anchor'd safe and sound, its voyage closed and done,
From fearful trip the victor ship comes in with object won;

Exult O shores, and ring O bells!
But I with mournful tread,
Walk the deck my Captain lies,
Fallen cold and dead.

Walt Whitman

Notes for **"Battle Hymn of the Republic"**

As an alternate lyric to a popular song of the Union Army "John Brown's Body," Julia Ward Howe wrote "The Battle Hymn of the Republic" during the Civil War in November, 1861. The song was then published in the *Atlantic Monthly* in February, 1862 and soon was adopted as a marching song by the Union Army. It has since become a favorite patriotic song in the United States.

The "grapes of wrath" refers to the anger of God, possibly from a passage in the *Book of Revelations 14:19-20*: "So the angel swung his sickle to the earth land gathered the clusters from the vine of the earth, and threw them into the great wine press of the wrath of God." — or from *Isaiah 63:3*: "I have trodden the winepress alone; from the nations no one was with me. I trampled them in my anger and trod them down in my wrath; their blood spattered my garments..."

John Steinbeck used the same reference to title his 1939 Pulitzer Prize novel *The Grapes of Wrath*. *The Grapes of Wrath* is a story about a tenant-farmer family, escaping the "Dust Bowl" drought years (three waves between 1934~1940) of economic hardship, agricultural changes and bank foreclosures; finally fleeing to California to seek work, land and their dignity. Other lyricists, such as Woody Guthrie, Pete Seeger and Bruce Springsteen (*The Ghost of Tom Joad* 1995), most recently have similarly given uplifting and supportive voices to the impoverished and unemployed people of our times. Harkening back to the Union Army's popular song "John Brown's Body," Bob Dylan's song "John Brown" too is a poignant testament to veterans disabled and traumatized by the wrath of war.

Another favorite, patriotic American song – originally written as a poem in 1895 – is "America the Beautiful," written by yet another woman Katharine Lee Bates, who like Julia Ward Howe, still inspires many Americans today.

**"Mine eyes have seen the glory
of the coming of the Lord:..."**

"His truth is marching on."

Battle Hymn of the Republic

Mine eyes have seen the glory of the coming of the Lord:
He is trampling out the vintage
  where the grapes of wrath are stored;
He hath loosed the fateful lightning
  of His terrible swift sword:
His truth is marching on.

**(Chorus)   Glory, glory, hallelujah!
    Glory, glory, hallelujah!
    Glory, glory, hallelujah!
      His truth is marching on.**
I have seen Him in the watch-fires
  of a hundred circling camps;
They have builded Him an altar
  in the evening dews and damps;
I can read His righteous sentence
  by the dim and flaring lamps.
His Day is marching on.
(Chorus)   Glory, glory, hallelujah! (etc.)
  His day is marching on.

I have read a fiery gospel
  writ in burnished rows of steel:
"As ye deal with my contemners,
  so with you my grace shall deal;
Let the Hero, born of woman,
  crush the serpent with his heel,
Since God is marching on."

Notes for **"Battle Hymn"** (cont.)

Julia Ward Howe (1819~1910) was an American poet and activist. She was not only an abolitionist but also a leader in the feminist movements in the later 1800s. She was president of the American Woman Suffrage Association. Although remembered today only for the "The Battle Hymn of the Republic," Howe was a noted poet and the first woman to be elected to the American Academy of Arts and Letters.

(**Chorus**) Glory, glory, hallelujah! (etc.)
              Since God is marching on.

He has sounded forth the trumpet
              that shall never call retreat;
He is sifting out the hearts of men
              before His judgment-seat:
Oh, be swift, my soul, to answer Him!
              be jubilant, my feet!
Our God is marching on.
(**Chorus**) Glory, glory, hallelujah! (etc.)
              Our God is marching on.

In the beauty of the lilies
              Christ was born across the sea,
With a glory in His bosom
              that transfigures you and me:
*As He died to make men holy,
              let us die to make men free,
While God is marching on.
(**Chorus**) Glory, glory, hallelujah!
          Glory, glory, hallelujah!
          Glory, glory, hallelujah!
              While God is marching on.

Julia Ward Howe

* Most recent performances substitute: "As He died to make men holy, let us *live* to make men free,...." for the lyric as originally written.

Notes for **"Dover Beach"**

This poem begins with the poet overlooking the beach and straits of the English Channel on a calm night and entreating his lover to join him at the window. They observe small inlet waves in the moonlight, as a French coastal lighthouse's beacon sweeps, "gleams and is gone" in the distance. From light-to-dark, wave-flung and withdrawn pebbles-to-people, and silence-to-a-roar, Matthew Arnold takes the reader from serene scene to the waves' ceaseless sounds that reveal "a thought."

Does "faith," if only even ours alone in each other, as Arnold intimates, keep at bay "the eternal note of sadness;" the same "turbid ebb and flow of human misery" the Greek dramatist and playwright Sophocles (496~406 BCE) too must have heard on the Aegean Sea?

Why do those white and pure cliffs of Dover then become "...vast edges drear and naked shingles of the world," against which waves beat a cadence of the "struggle and flight" of "ignorant armies" clashing by night?

Matthew Arnold sets forth an explosive analogy for the importance of personal commitment alongside a world seemingly surrendering faith, then receding and declining into decadence. Our faith in being "true to one another" is to a vast glimmering, folded-in-a-bright-girdle, tranquil bay as the withdrawing and retreating world-faith is to the "grating roar" of no joy, no light, and no peace on a "darkling — 'ever-darkening' — plain" of waves before us. The poet seems to retreat inward, finding no joy or light in the world, and his analogy is to a plain "where ignorant armies clash by night." That is, various factions and parties, who have not any depth of knowledge about their own beliefs, blindly contend with each other.

What of our own beliefs in each other? Are they more secure, more full of joy, love and light?

MATTHEW ARNOLD

"Where ignorant armies clash by night."

Dover Beach

The sea is calm tonight.
The tide is full, the moon lies fair
Upon the straits; on the French coast the light
Gleams and is gone; the cliffs of England stand,
Glimmering and vast, out in the tranquil bay.
Come to the window, sweet is the night-air!
Only, from the long line of spray
Where the sea meets the moon-blanched land,
Listen! you hear the grating roar
Of pebbles which the waves draw back, and fling,
At their return, up the high strand,
Begin, and cease, and then again begin,
With tremulous cadence slow, and bring
The eternal note of sadness in.

Sophocles long ago
Heard it on the Ægean, and it brought
Into his mind the turbid ebb and flow
Of human misery; we
Find also in the sound a thought,
Hearing it by this distant northern sea.

Notes for **"Dover Beach"** (cont.)

Matthew Arnold (1822~1888), critic, poet, and essayist, is considered the shaper of English criticism during the mid-to-late nineteenth century. He defined "criticism" in his essay "The Function of Criticism at the Present Time" in *Essays in Criticism* (1865-1888) as "a disinterested endeavour to learn and propagate the best that is known and thought in the world."

Arnold was particularly concerned with maintaining culture in an age of democracy and industrialization. Seeing literature as the shaper and sustainer of culture, Matthew Arnold urged more study of the classics, using the lines and expressions of the great masters as "touchstones" to evaluate good writing. His most famous poems are "Dover Beach" (1867) and "The Scholar Gypsy" (1853).

The Sea of Faith
Was once, too, at the full, and round earth's shore
Lay like the folds of a bright girdle furled.
But now I only hear
Its melancholy, long, withdrawing roar,
Retreating, to the breath
Of the night-wind, down the vast edges drear
And naked shingles of the world.

Ah, love, let us be true
To one another! for the world, which seems
To lie before us like a land of dreams,
So various, so beautiful, so new,
Hath really neither joy, nor love, nor light,
Nor certitude, nor peace, nor help for pain;
And we are here as on a darkling plain
Swept with confused alarms of struggle and flight,
Where ignorant armies clash by night.

Matthew Arnold

Notes for **"No Frigate Like a Book"**

This poem is not complicated, but the imagery is quite elaborate for a statement about something as commonplace as either words in a book or poetry on a page. Both a "frigate" and "coursers" carry or "bear" their cargo, which in this case would be readers of books and poetry. Thus, what does the poet say about books and poetry in the first stanza? Additionally, the word "traverse," as noted above, can also mean a "journey" or a "passage." As you, the reader of this poem, travel into the second stanza, what then does the poet have to add about books and poetry? Have you too been afforded a chance to ride in a Chariot (of words) pulled by coursers to Lands away?

If not, and you would like a little more familiarity with rhyme, rhythm, and how words can indeed allow a traverse with prancing coursers — in this case reindeer, try reading Clement Clarke Moore's "A Visit from St. Nicholas" ('Twas the Night Before Christmas) first published in 1823.

Emily Dickinson (1830~1886) was an eccentric but great American poet who lived in Amherst, Massachusetts. She studied at the Amherst Academy for seven years in her youth and then spent a short time at Mount Holyoke Female Seminary before returning to her family's house in Amherst where she lived a reclusive life, seldom visiting with anyone. She always wore white clothing and was reluctant to greet guests or, later in life, even to leave her room. Most of her friendships were therefore carried out by correspondence.

Many scholars and students of poetry have commented on Emily Dickinson's focus on the life beyond our own temporal physical existences, and her vehicles (here books) for transport to other worlds have always been interesting. One of her best-known, often-recited poems with a similar, yet perhaps darker, passage to other worlds is entitled: "Because I could not stop for death – (479)."

The noted critic Harold Bloom considers Walt Whitman and Emily Dickinson "the two greatest and most original of American poets." "Like Whitman's," Bloom has written, "Dickinson's poetry looks simple and is very difficult."

There is no Frigate like a Book

There is no Frigate like a Book*
To take us Lands away
Nor any Coursers like a Page *
Of prancing Poetry –

This Traverse may the poorest take*
Without oppress of Toll –*
How frugal is the Chariot*
That bears the Human Soul –

Emily Dickinson

* **Frigate** = a large long distance merchant ship
* **Coursers** = horses bred for racing or battle
* **traverse** = journey
* **toll** = cost or money
* **frugal** = low-priced, economical

Notes for **"Jabberwocky"**

"Jabberwocky" (probably Lewis Carroll's most famous nonsense poem) is from *Through the Looking Glass* written in 1894. The opening stanza of "Jabberwocky" was first published in an 1855 edition of the periodical *Mischmasch*, a publication Lewis Carroll wrote and illustrated for the amusement of his family. This first stanza is the verse Humpty Dumpty explains to Alice in *Through the Looking Glass*. Lewis Carroll added the other verses years later during a verse-making game with his cousins.

The word 'jabberwocky' itself means "invented or meaningless language; nonsense," so the periodical's German name, *Mischmasch*, from "mish mash"– meaning 'a disorderly mixture of things' – seems a most appropriate repository for Carroll's mish mash of words. For example, in "Jabberwocky," "frumious" is a mish mash of the words 'fuming' and 'furious,' while "burble" is a mish mash of 'bleat,' 'murmur' and 'warble.' Some of Carroll's mashed-up words in "Jabberwocky" did, however, make it into the *Oxford English Dictionary*: "galumph" – a combination of 'gallop' and 'triumphant,' along with "chortled" – a mish mash of 'chuckle' and 'snort.'

Lewis Carroll (1832~1898), whose original birth name was Charles Lutwidge Dodgson, was a professor of Mathematics at Christ Church College in Oxford, England. He wrote many poems but is most famous for his novels *Alice in Wonderland* and *Through the Looking Glass*.

"Beware the Jabberwock, my son!"

Jabberwocky

'Twas brillig, and the slithy toves
Did gyre and gimble in the wabe:
All mimsy were the borogoves,
And the mome raths outgrabe.

"Beware the Jabberwock, my son!
The jaws that bite, the claws that catch!
Beware the Jubjub bird, and shun
The frumious Bandersnatch!"

He took his vorpal sword in hand:
Long time the manxome foe he sought —
So rested he by the Tumtum tree,
And stood awhile in thought.

And, as in uffish thought he stood,
The Jabberwock, with eyes of flame,
Came whiffling through the tulgey wood,
And burbled as it came!

One, two! One, two! And through and through
The vorpal blade went snicker-snack!
He left it dead, and with its head
He went galumphing back.

"And, has thou slain the Jabberwock?
Come to my arms, my beamish boy!
O frabjous day! Callooh! Callay!"
He chortled in his joy.

Lewis Carroll

Notes for **"God's Grandeur"**

Did you think Gerard Manley Hopkins woke up one morning and saw the spectacular, ever-widening wings of a sunrise?

In this poem, "God's Grandeur," a sonnet written in 1877, Hopkins first faithfully acknowledges the all-pervasive and omnipresent hand of the creator, comparing it both to a shaken foil's flash of light and next to the ooze of oil that, even when crushed (displaced), gathers again its 'greatness' either at the edges of any pressure exerted upon it or when, for example, olives yield the ooze of olive oil when crushed. Remembering how God's grandeur "gathers to a greatness like the ooze of oil crushed," analogously the bright and warm, morning sun too, breaking through and around a dirty sky, eventually "gathers to a greatness" during the day as well. How is it possible, Hopkins then asks, men cannot recognize God's Grandeur—his all-pervasive authority and presence in our world?

Next, through assonance (repetition of vowel sounds) and alliteration (repetition of consonant sounds), Hopkins presents the problem of mankind's continued steps of ruinous development that distance even his own, now "shod" footsteps from feeling the now bare soil:

> *Generations have trod, have trod, have trod;*
> *And all is seared with trade; bleared, smeared with toil;*
> *And wears man's smudge and shares man's smell: the soil*
> *Is bare now, nor can foot feel, being shod.*

"The world is charged with the grandeur of God."

God's Grandeur

The world is charged with the grandeur of God.
It will flame out, like shining from shook foil;*
It gathers to a greatness, like the ooze of oil
Crushed. Why do men then now not reck his rod?*
Generations have trod, have trod, have trod;
And all is seared with trade; bleared, smeared with toil;
And wears man's smudge and shares man's smell: the soil
Is bare now, nor can foot feel, being shod.*
And for all this, nature is never spent;
There lives the dearest freshness deep down things;
And though the last lights off the black West went
Oh, morning, at the brown brink eastward, springs —
Because the Holy Ghost over the bent
World broods with warm breast and with ah! bright wings*

Gerard Manley Hopkins

* **foil** = a kind of sword used in fencing — when the sword is shaken it will flash. It also could mean a sheet of thin metal foil that when shaken will flash and shine
* **reck** = "recognize" or "pay attention to"
  rod = authority
* **nor can foot feel, being shod** - we wear shoes and can't feel the earth
* **to brood** (verb) = to sit upon eggs to be hatched, as a bird

Notes for **"God's Grandeur"** (cont.)

Yet Hopkins in the final stanza is hopeful because, in spite of man for generations having "smudged" the world, "nature is never spent." Recalling not only "the dearest freshness deep down things" but also the "spring" of the bright, morning sun, even "at the brown brink eastward" (sooty, polluted, eastward sky's edge), Hopkins assures the reader that this "Holy Ghost" (as the sun) – the messenger of God's grandeur – will still arise daily and, like a mother bird, rest warmly upon the egg of this "bent world" to nurture it.

It is interesting to compare this sonnet with Wordsworth's sonnet: "The World is Too Much With Us." There are two sonnet structures from which all other sonnets in the English language are formed: Petrarchan and Shakespearean. Sonnets are fourteen-line poems, where the octet (the first eight lines) usually presents a problem and the sestet (the next six lines) offers a solution.

Gerard Manley Hopkins (1844~1899), an English poet, was a Jesuit priest. His poems have very unusual rhythms and were considered quite advanced for his time (the Victorian Era when Queen Victoria was Queen of England). His poems reflect both his love of nature and his worry about industry taking over the world. Most of his poems are short, but his most famous work is a long poem called "The Wreck of the Deutschland" (1875).

Notes for **"The New Colossus"**

* **twin cities** = Brooklyn and New York City which, at that time, had not yet been consolidated as one city.

* **-tost** = tossed, as in hit repeatedly by storms and troubles while crossing the oceans; hence, 'tempest-tost.'

"The New Colossus" is an allusion to the famous statue, the Colossus of Rhodes, constructed in that city in 280 BCE to celebrate the island and City of Rhodes' freedom from Cyprus in 305 BCE. It is considered one of the Seven Wonders of the Ancient World.

Neither the sculptor Frederic-Auguste Bartholdi nor the donor France intended the gift of the Statute of Liberty to America to be a symbol welcoming immigrants from across the ocean. But Emma Lazarus' sonnet, along with waves of immigrant ships passing below Miss Liberty, quickly established its meaning for millions of emigrants looking for a "door" to new beginnings in America.

One also might want to compare and contrast this sculpted "new colossus" with both Percy Bysshe Shelley's "legs of stone" in "Ozymandias" and the "beast" that "slouches towards Bethlehem to be born" in William Butler Yeats' "The Second Coming" — both found in this collection.

Emma Lazarus (1849~1887) was an American poet and translator who lived in New York City. She is best remembered for this sonnet, which in 1903 was inscribed on a plaque placed on the pedestal of the Statue of Liberty, located on Liberty Island in New York Harbor.

**"Give me your tired, your poor,
Your huddled masses yearning to breathe free,…."**

The New Colossus

Not like the brazen giant of Greek fame,
With conquering limbs astride from land to land;
Here at our sea-washed, sunset gates shall stand
A mighty woman with a torch, whose flame
Is the imprisoned lightning, and her name
Mother of Exiles. From her beacon-hand
Glows world-wide welcome; her mild eyes command
The air-bridged harbor that twin cities frame.*
"Keep, ancient lands, your storied pomp!" cries she
With silent lips. "Give me your tired, your poor,
Your huddled masses yearning to breathe free,
The wretched refuse of your teeming shore.
Send these, the homeless, tempest-tost to me,*
I lift my lamp beside the golden door!"

Emma Lazarus

Notes for **"Invictus"**

"Invictus" means "unconquerable or invincible." The theme of the poem is the will to survive in face of all difficulties and the fact that death is inevitable. The poem is favored by those who see themselves as masters of their own fate in a world that does not care for the individual. Critics say the poem is melodramatic, but no one denies its eloquence.

Nelson Mandela is said to have recited the poem to other prisoners when he was incarcerated at Robben Island prison, and the last stanza was both quoted by Barack Obama at Mandela's memorial service in December, 2013 and reprinted on the December 14, 2013 cover of *The Economist* magazine. The line "bloody but unbowed" was the headline in the *London Daily Mirror* after the July 7th, 2005 London public transportation system bombings.

Henley wrote the poem in 1875 and published it in 1888 with no title. In later printings the poem was titled "I.M. R.T. Hamilton Bruce (1846 -1899)," that is, 'In Memory (of) R.T. Hamilton Bruce,' who was a Scotsman and flour importer, interested in the arts and co-founder of *The Scots Observer* to which he appointed his friend William Earnest Henley as editor. First published in Edinburgh in 1889, the magazine later moved to London and became *The National Observer.* When the poem was finally included in *The Oxford Book of English Verse*, the title "Invictus" was added by the then editor Arthur Quiller-Couch.

William Earnest Henley (1849~1903) was an English poet who as a child had one of his legs amputated due to tubercular arthritis. Although editor of influential British magazines of the day, Henley's fame rests on this one poem written in Scotland in 1875, where he was recovering from then radical, multiple operations to save his other leg. Henley was a close friend of both Robert Louis Stevenson and Rudyard Kipling, and in "Invictus," one can find a bit of the kind of courage Kipling wrote about in his poem "If—." Melodramatic or not, Henley was no doubt courageous in the face of a disease that almost took both his legs.

"My head is bloody, but unbowed"

**"I am the master of my fate,
I am the captain of my soul."**

Invictus
I.M. R.T. Hamilton Bruce (1846 -1899)

Out of the night that covers me,
Black as the pit from pole to pole,
I thank whatever gods may be
For my unconquerable soul.

In the fell clutch of circumstance
I have not winced nor cried aloud.
Under the bludgeonings of chance
My head is bloody, but unbowed.

Beyond this place of wrath and tear
Looms but the Horror of the shade
And yet the menace of the years
Finds and shall find me unafraid.

It matters not how strait the gate,
How charged with punishments the scroll,
I am the master of my fate,
I am the captain of my soul.

William Earnest Henley

Notes for **"Requiem"**

Robert Louis Stevenson composed these lines in 1880 when he was ill in California. They now appear on his tombstone on the top of Mount Vaea overlooking Apia, the capital of Samoa. The Samoans called him "Tusitala" or 'the teller of tales.'

The quoted lines: "Home is the sailor, home from the sea, and the hunter home from the hill," are often erroneously attributed to the British poet A.E. Housman (1859-1936) who, sometime after 1922, wrote a tribute to Stevenson titled "XXII R.L.S." The first line of Housman's poem is:

> *Home is the sailor, home from sea:*
> *** and the last lines are ***
> *Home is the sailor from the sea,*
> *The hunter from the hill.*

Note in Stevenson's poem his use of the word "will," which may refer to a request after death — as in the 'writing of a will.' Next, observe the word "grave," used here by Stevenson in both its noun and verb forms. The latter, verb-form for "grave" means to "carve, sculpt or engrave," and so here Stevenson — almost perpetually in "grave" health (the adjective-form of the word) himself — asks in his "will" to have someone "grave" these words above his "grave," where he will repose, or ultimately rest.

Robert Louis Stevenson (1850~1894), a Scottish novelist and poet, born in Edinburgh in 1850, was primarily a novelist who wrote *Treasure Island, Kidnapped,* and *The Strange Case of Dr. Jekyll and Mr. Hyde.* In 1885 he also published a volume of very popular poetry: *A Child's Garden of Verses.*

ROBERT LEWIS STEVENSON

**"Home is the sailor, home from the sea,
And the hunter home from the hill."**

Requiem

Under the wide and starry sky,
Dig the grave and let me lie.
Glad did I live and gladly die,
And I laid me down with a will.
This be the verse you grave for me:
Here he lies where he longed to be;
Home is the sailor, home from sea,
And the hunter home from the hill.

Robert Louis Stevenson

Notes for **"The Ballad of Reading Gaol"**

* **gaol** = jail

This is a long poem (original 654 lines, shorter version 576 lines) reflecting the two years that Oscar Wilde spent in prison, where, among witnessing other events, he watched a man waiting to be hanged for killing his wife. In this poem Wilde tries to convey the roughness and monotony of prison life in an attempt to plead for prison reform.

Wilde wrote the poem in 1898 just after he was released from prison, where he had been sentenced to two years of hard labor for homosexual activity. The poem was first published under his prisoner identification number, C.3-3.

The poem is about the imprisonment and hanging on Tuesday, July 7, 1896 of Charles Thomas Woolridge, who was convicted of cutting the throat of his wife Laura Ellen. Wooldridge had been a trooper in the Royal Horse Guards, and as a trooper he wore a "scarlet coat."

The memorable line: "And all men kill the thing they love,…" may have its precursor in Shakespeare's *Merchant of Venice* (Act 4; Scene 1) in the interchange between Bassanio and Shylock, when Bassanio criticizes Shylock for demanding his "pound of flesh" from Antonio:

BASSANIO: "Do all men kill the things they do not love?"
SHYLOCK: "Hates any man the thing he would not kill?"
BASSANIO: "Every offence is not a hate at first."

Also in regard to "And all men kill the thing they love,…" the second to last line in this poem suggests "The coward does it with a kiss,….". Here Oscar Wilde reminds his audience that Jesus Christ was betrayed with a kiss by Judas Iscariot, one of Christ's original twelve disciples.

"And all men kill the thing they love,…."

The Ballad of Reading Gaol*

***** = lines omitted

I

He did not wear his scarlet coat,
  For blood and wine are red,
And blood and wine were on his hands
  When they found him with the dead,
The poor dead woman whom he loved,
  And murdered in her bed.

He walked amongst the Trial Men
  In a suit of shabby grey;
A cricket cap was on his head,
  And his step seemed light and gay;
But I never saw a man who looked
  So wistfully at the day.

I never saw a man who looked
  With such a wistful eye
Upon that little tent of blue
  Which prisoners call the sky,
And at every drifting cloud that went
  With sails of silver by.

I walked, with other souls in pain,
  Within another ring,
And was wondering if the man had done
  A great or little thing,
When a voice behind me whispered low,
"That fellow's got to swing."
*****

Notes for **"The Ballad of Reading Gaol"** (cont.)

This poem is in traditional ballad form. Ballads are among the oldest forms of oral recitation in the English language; meant to preserve stories from generation to generation.

The typical ballad alternates four stress and three stress lines (usually iambic tetrameter followed by iambic trimeter). Although most ballads have four lines rhymed **a-b-c-b** (see Coleridge's *Rime of the Ancient Mariner* and the folk story about John Henry), in this poem Wilde uses a six-line ballad rhyming **a-b-c-b-d-b.**

Oscar Wilde (October 16, 1854~November 30, 1900) was an Irish novelist, playwright, and poet. Today he is remembered for his epigrams, his novel *The Picture of Dorian Gray,* his plays: *The Importance of Being Earnest* and *Lady Windemere's Fan,* his children's stories, such as *The Selfish Giant,* and his poetry, such as "De Profundus" and "The Ballad of Reading Gaol." After his time in prison, he was physically and emotionally drained and without money. He moved to Paris and died within a year-and-a-half of leaving prison.

V

I know not whether laws be right,
    Or whether laws be wrong;
All we know who lie in gaol
    Is that the wall is strong;
And each day is like a year,
    A year whose days are long.
        *****

VI

In Reading gaol by Reading town
    There is a pit of shame,
And in it lies a wretched man
    Eaten by the teeth of flame,
In a burning winding-sheet he lies,
    And his grave has got no name.

And there, till Christ call forth the dead,
    In silence let him lie:
No need to waste the foolish tear,
    Or heave the windy sigh:
The man had killed the thing he loved,
    And so he had to die.

And all men kill the thing they love,
    By all let this be heard,
Some do it with a bitter look,
    Some with a flattering word,
The coward does it with a kiss,
    The brave man with a sword!

Oscar Wilde

Notes for **"The House by the Side of the Road"**

This poem, with its measured, flowing rhythm, straightforward themes and common language, was the type of easily-learned verse Sam Walter Foss used to appeal to the general public, writing a poem a day for the newspapers. We can say that Sam Walter Foss always kept his audience in mind when he wrote!

Foss also wrote "The Coming American" which has been widely quoted. The first of its three stanzas reads:

The Coming American

Bring me men to match my mountains,
Bring me men to match my plains,
Men with empires in their purpose,
And new eras in their brains.
Bring me men to match my prairies,
Men to match my inland seas,
Men whose thoughts shall pave a highway
Up to ampler destinies,
Pioneers to cleanse thought's marshlands,
And to cleanse old error's fen;
Bring me men to match my mountains –
Bring me men!

The first line of this poem: "Bring me men to match my mountains" is engraved on the Jesse Unruh State Office Building in Sacramento, California. Irving Stone used the phrase as the title to his 1956 book *Men to Match My Mountains: The Opening of the Far West 1840-1900.*

**"Let me live in a house by the side of the road
And be a friend to man."**

The House by the Side of the Road

There are hermit souls that live withdrawn
In the place of their self-content;
There are souls like stars, that dwell apart,
In a fellowless firmament;
There are pioneer souls that blaze the paths
Where highways never ran-
But let me live by the side of the road
And be a friend to man.

Let me live in a house by the side of the road
Where the race of men go by-
The men who are good and the men who are bad,
As good and as bad as I.
I would not sit in the scorner's seat
Nor hurl the cynic's ban-
Let me live in a house by the side of the road
And be a friend to man.

I see from my house by the side of the road
By the side of the highway of life,
The men who press with the ardor of hope,
The men who are faint with the strife,
But I turn not away from their smiles and tears,
Both parts of an infinite plan-
Let me live in a house by the side of the road
And be a friend to man.

Notes for **"The House by the Side of the Road"**
(cont.)

Sam Walter Foss (June 19, 1858~February 26, 1911) was an American librarian and poet. He was born in New Hampshire and graduated from Brown University. He is best known for "The House By the Side of the Road."

I know there are brook-gladdened meadows ahead,
And mountains of wearisome height;
That the road passes on through the long afternoon
And stretches away to the night.
And still I rejoice when the travelers rejoice
And weep with the strangers that moan,
Nor live in my house by the side of the road
Like a man who dwells alone.

Let me live in my house by the side of the road,
Where the race of men go by-
They are good, they are bad,
    they are weak, they are strong,
Wise, foolish - so am I.
Then why should I sit in the scorner's seat,
Or hurl the cynic's ban?
Let me live in my house by the side of the road
And be a friend to man.

Sam Walter Foss

Notes for **"Oranges and Lemons"**

This poem begins with the bells of St. Clement's church; across the street from which there was a wharf (dock) where citrus-fruit cargoes from the Mediterranean were delivered. It is said the church bells pealed (rang out) when a cargo arrived.

St Martin's refers to a church on Martin's Lane, a street where there were once many moneylenders.

Old Bailey was a famous prison. Debtors (persons who owed money) were often put there. It was also known as Newgate Prison.

Shoreditch was an area of London once known for its poverty but is now a quite fashionable area of London.

The church at Stepney was known as the "Church of the High Seas." Many sailors were buried in the churchyard. The phrase "When will that be?" could possibly refer to wives waiting for their sailors to return from voyages with their fortunes, or, as the old saying goes, "waiting for their ship to come in."

Also known as "Bow Church," St. Mary-le-Bow Church is in Cheapside, London. During the fourteenth century a curfew was rung on the Bow Bells every night at 9 p.m. These lines probably mean that the poem is finished.

Finally, there is a tradition that anyone born within hearing distance of Bow Bells ringing is a true Cockney: a "Bow-bell Cockney."

"Oranges and lemons say the bells of St. Clement's"

Oranges and Lemons

Oranges and lemons
Say the bells of St. Clement's

You owe me five farthings,
Say the bells of St. Martin's

When will you pay me?
Say the bells of Old Bailey

When I grow rich,
Say the bells of Shoreditch

When will that be?
Say the bells of Stepney

I'm sure I don't know,
Says the great bell of Bow

— *An anonymous poem (nursery rhyme)
about the church bells of London*

Notes for **"John Henry"**

This is just one of many versions of a song about the legend of a man named John Henry who, the stories say, worked on the railroads either in West Virginia or Alabama. His job was to pound steel rods into the rock so that the holes he made could be filled with dynamite to blast rock away and tracks could be laid for railroads.

In the middle of the 1800s a steam drill was invented to drive the steel railroad spikes. The steam drill would eventually replace the men. Men like John Henry, of course, did not want to lose their jobs, so they challenged the steam drill. But they could not succeed.

The "shaker" is the man who holds the railroad spike while the driver hits the spike with a sledgehammer. Can you figure out why he is called the "shaker"?

For other musical versions of this song, listen to either Woody Guthrie or Doc Watson or Joe Bonamassa perform "John Henry" on YouTube.

The author of this ballad is unknown.

**"Here lies a steel drivin' man, Lord, Lord.
Here lies a steel drivin' man."**

Ballad of John Henry

When John Henry was a little baby,
Sitting on his pappy's knee,
He picked up a hammer and a little piece of steel,
He said, "This hammer'll be the death of me, Lord,
Lord.
 This hammer'll be the death of me."

Now, the captain said to John Henry,
"I'm gonna bring that steam drill around.
I'm gonna take that steam drill out on the job,
I'm gonna whop that steel on down, Lord, Lord.
 Gonna whop that steel on down."

John Henry said to his captain,
"A man ain't nothing but a man,
But before I let that steam drill beat me down,
I'll die with my hammer in my hand, Lord, Lord.
 I'll die with my hammer in my hand."

John Henry said to his shaker,
"Shaker, you better pray
'Cause if I miss this six foot of steel
Tomorrow'll be your burying day, Lord, Lord
 Tomorrow'll be your burying day."

WHOSE WORDS THESE ARE

The man who invented the steam drill,
He thought he was mighty fine.
But John Henry drove fourteen feet
And the steam drill only drove nine, Lord, Lord.
  The steam drill only drove nine.

John Henry hammered on the mountain
His hammer was striking fire.
He hammered so hard that he broke his poor heart.
He laid down his hammer and he died, Lord, Lord.
  He laid down his hammer and he died.

They took John Henry to the graveyard,
And buried him down in the sand.
Now every locomotive that comes a-rolling by
Says, "Here lies a steel-driving man, Lord, Lord.
  Here lies a steel-driving man."

author unknown

Notes for **"Casey at the Bat"**

Apart from this poem being about a truly American sport, derived from the English games of rounders and cricket, this poem achieves what Edgar Allen Poe called "the unity of effect," which he strove thematically for in all his own poems and short stories (see "The Raven" in this collection).

In the build-up to Casey coming to bat in the ninth inning, note how the author sets into motion a rising tension and anticipation, which includes where, when, how, who, what and why, that culminates abruptly and ultimately in disappointment. While we have all had this kind of sudden let-down after diligent preparation to succeed in our lives, good writing includes answers to the aforementioned *Wh*-questions. And even at the sentence-level of writing, if a writer can include enough detail to answer as many of the *Wh*-questions as possible, s/he will have written an interesting sentence that moves not only the prose/verse itself but also her/his reader. Here the author, not only by employing a steady, two-line end-rhyme scheme in each four-line verse but also by offering-up specific *Wh*-question details throughout the story, achieves Poe's "unity of effect" while accurately chronicling the action; then accelerating the intensity, joy and sometimes heartbreak found in a truly great American sport.

ERNEST LAWRENCE THAYER

"...there is no joy in Mudville"

Casey at the Bat

The outlook wasn't brilliant for the Mudville nine that day;
The score stood four to two with one inning left to play.
And then when Cooney died at first, and Barrows did the same,
A sickly silence fell upon the patrons of the game.

A straggling few got up to go in deep despair. The rest
Clung to that hope which springs eternal in the human breast;
They thought if only Casey could but get a whack at that —
We'd put up even money now with Casey at the bat.

But Flynn preceded Casey, as did also Jimmy Blake,
And the former was a lulu and the latter was a cake;
So upon that stricken multitude grim melancholy sat,
For there seemed but little chance of Casey's getting to the bat.

But Flynn let drive a single, to the wonderment of all,
And Blake, the much despised, tore the cover off the ball;
And when the dust had lifted, and men saw what had occurred,
There was Jimmy safe at second and Flynn a-hugging third.

Then from 5,000 throats and more there rose a lusty yell;
It rumbled through the valley, it rattled in the dell;
It knocked upon the mountain and recoiled upon the flat,
For Casey, mighty Casey, was advancing to the bat.

There was ease in Casey's manner as he stepped into his place;
There was pride in Casey's bearing and a smile on Casey's face.
And when, responding to the cheers, he lightly doffed his hat,
No stranger in the crowd could doubt 'twas Casey at the bat.

Ten thousand eyes were on him as he rubbed his hands with dirt;
Five thousand tongues applauded when he wiped them on his shirt.
Then while the writhing pitcher ground the ball into his hip,
Defiance gleamed in Casey's eye, a sneer curled Casey's lip.

Notes for **"Casey at the Bat"** (cont.)

Ernest Lawrence Thayer (August 14, 1863~August 21, 1940) was an American writer and poet, who graduated from Harvard University in 1885 and followed his Harvard friend William Randolph Hearst to write for the *San Francisco Examiner*. Thayer often contributed ballads to the Sunday edition of the newspaper and in 1888 wrote "Casey at the Bat."

According to the *Baseball Almanac*, "Casey at the Bat" is "...the most famous baseball poem ever written."

And now the leather-covered sphere came hurtling through the air,
And Casey stood a-watching it in haughty grandeur there.
Close by the sturdy batsman the ball unheeded sped —
"That ain't my style," said Casey. "Strike one," the umpire said.

From the benches, filled with people, there went up a muffled roar,
Like the beating of the storm-waves on a stern and distant shore.
"Kill him! Kill the umpire!" shouted someone in the stand;
And it's likely they'd have killed him had not Casey raised his hand.

With a smile of Christian charity great Casey's visage shone;
He stilled the rising tumult; he bade the game go on;
He signaled to the pitcher, and once more the spheroid flew;
But Casey still ignored it, and the umpire said, "Strike two."

"Fraud!" cried the maddened thousands, and echo answered "fraud;"
But one scornful look from Casey and the audience was awed.
They saw his face grow stern and cold, they saw his muscles strain,
And they knew that Casey wouldn't let that ball go by again.

The sneer is gone from Casey's lip, his teeth are clinched in hate;
He pounds with cruel violence his bat upon the plate.
And now the pitcher holds the ball, and now he lets it go,
And now the air is shattered by the force of Casey's blow.

Oh, somewhere in this favored land the sun is shining bright;
The band is playing somewhere, and somewhere hearts are light,
And somewhere men are laughing, and somewhere children shout;
But there is no joy in Mudville — mighty Casey has struck out.

Ernest Lawrence Thayer

Notes for **"Gunga Din"**

The speaker in this poem is a British soldier serving in India when India was ruled by England. He seems to be talking to some new army recruits. The soldier says that a combatant needs water when he fights and must rely on the regimental water carriers (the "bhisti"). The soldier tells of his admiration for Gunga Din, a native water-carrier who saved the soldier's life and then lost his own.

The speaker reflects the racist views of the poet and perhaps others in the British army at the time who viewed the natives as a lower order. They called the bhisti "the blackfaced crew." Then ambiguously, with respect to Gunga Din, the poet reflects both his racism and admirations as he says : "An' for all 'is dirty 'ide / 'E was white, clear white, inside." And at the end he reflects an appreciation of their common humanity when he says, "You're a better man than I am, Gunga Din."

"Common humanity" would suggest, for all our overall emphasis on independence and individualism, we are forever dependent upon other individuals and the collective strength of the diverse communities in which we live — a view not lost on Kipling as he completes this poem.

There are several recited versions of this poem, as well as the classic, 1939 movie of the same name starring Cary Grant, which is available on YouTube.

"You're a better man than I am, Gunga Din!"

Gunga Din

You may talk o' gin and beer
When you're quartered safe out 'ere,
An' you're sent to penny-fights an' Aldershot it;
But when it comes to slaughter
You will do your work on water,
An' you'll lick the bloomin' boots of 'im that's got it.
Now in Injia's sunny clime,
Where I used to spend my time
A-servin' of 'Er Majesty the Queen,
Of all them blackfaced crew
The finest man I knew
Was our regimental bhisti, Gunga Din,

      He was 'Din! Din! Din!
      'You limpin' lump o' brick-dust, Gunga Din!
      'Hi! Slippy *hitherao*
      'Water, get it! Panee *lao*,
      'You squidgy-nosed old idol, Gunga Din.'

The uniform 'e wore
Was nothin' much before,
An' rather less than 'arf o' that be'ind,
For a piece o' twisty rag
An' a goatskin water-bag
Was all the field-equipment 'e could find.
When the sweatin' troop-train lay
In a sidin' through the day,
Where the 'eat would make your bloomin' eyebrows
      crawl,
We shouted 'Harry By!'
Till our throats were bricky-dry,
Then we wopped 'im 'cause 'e couldn't serve us all.

Notes for **"Gunga Din"** (cont.)

Rudyard Kipling (1865~1936) was a British novelist, short story writer and poet, who was born in India and spent a good part of his life there. He was the first British writer to be awarded the Nobel Prize for literature. He is known for his belief that the British were superior and so should rule and "civilize" the world (see his poem "The White Man's Burden"), but he was also conscious of the impermanence of power as his poem "Recessional" shows. Among his other famous poems are "The Road to Mandalay" and "If–." Among his books are *Kim*, *The Jungle Book* and *Captains Courageous*. One of his famous short stories made into film was *The Man Who Would Be King*.

> It was 'Din! Din! Din!
> You 'eathen, where the mischief 'ave you been?
> 'You put some *juldee* in it
> 'Or I'll *marrow* you this minute
> 'If you don't fill up my helmet, Gunga Din!'

'E would dot an' carry one
Till the longest day was done;
An' 'e didn't seem to know the use o' fear.
If we charged or broke or cut,
You could bet your bloomin' nut,
'E'd be waitin' fifty paces right flank rear.
With 'is mussick on 'is back,
'E would skip with our attack,
An' watch us till the bugles made 'Retire,'
An' for all 'is dirty 'ide
'E was white, clear white, inside
When 'e went to tend the wounded under fire!

> It was 'Din! Din! Din!'
> With the bullets kickin' dust-spots on the green.
> When the cartridges ran out,
> You could hear the front-ranks shout,
> 'Hi! ammunition-mules an' Gunga Din!'

I shan't forgit the night
When I dropped be'ind the fight
With a bullet where my belt-plate should 'a' been.
I was chokin' mad with thirst,
An' the man that spied me first
Was our good old grinnin', gruntin' Gunga Din.
'E lifted up my 'ead,

WHOSE WORDS THESE ARE

An' he plugged me where I bled,
An' 'e guv me 'arf-a-pint o' water green.
It was crawlin' and it stunk,
But of all the drinks I've drunk,
I'm gratefullest to one from Gunga Din.

    It was 'Din! Din! Din!
    'Ere's a beggar with a bullet through 'is spleen;
    'E's chawin' up the ground,
     'An' 'e's kickin' all around:
    'For Gawd's sake git the water, Gunga Din!'

'E carried me away
To where a dooli lay,
An' a bullet come an' drilled the beggar clean.
'E put me safe inside,
An' just before 'e died,
'I 'ope you liked your drink,' sez Gunga Din.
So I'll meet 'im later on
At the place where 'e is gone —
Where it's always double drill and no canteen.
'E'll be squattin' on the coals
Givin' drink to poor damned souls,
An' I'll get a swig in hell from Gunga Din!

    Yes, Din! Din! Din!
    You Lazarushian-leather Gunga Din!
    Though I've belted you and flayed you,
    By the livin' Gawd that made you,
    You're a better man than I am, Gunga Din!

Rudyard Kipling

Notes for "If—"

Rudyard Kipling wrote this poem for his son John in 1910, listing the traits of a good man. Notice that the poet does not say that his son should try to be rich or famous. Rather, he says his son should be humble, patient, truthful, dependable and able to persevere. He should be able to work both with those who are great and those who are ordinary people. He should have faith in himself even when circumstances go bad, other people are cruel to him, tell lies about him, or twist his words.

The poem is about character, and character is defined as how you act when others are not observing you. Either read this poem aloud or silently to yourself, and sense how Kipling's "you" and all the following noble traits move you to apply those challenges to yourself. Keeping this poem in mind, find, reread, and again think about both Polonius' advice to his son Laertes on p. 37 and William Earnest Henley's message in "Invictus" on p. 233 in this collection. How do you define your own character and yourself in this world?

This poem is very famous in Britain. It almost defines what the British call "the stiff upper lip." (even when things go bad, do not let your mouth tremble and show it).

Rudyard Kipling (1865~1936) was a British novelist, short story writer and poet, who was born in India and spent a good part of his life there. He was the first British writer to be awarded the Nobel Prize for literature in 1907.

"If you can keep your head when all about you
Are losing theirs and blaming it on you;…."

If —

If you can keep your head when all about you
Are losing theirs and blaming it on you,
If you can trust yourself when all men doubt you,
But make allowance for their doubting too;
If you can wait and not be tired by waiting,
Or, being lied about, don't deal in lies,
Or being hated don't give way to hating,
And yet don't look too good, nor talk too wise:

If you can dream — and not make dreams your master;
If you can think — and not make thoughts your aim;
If you can meet with Triumph and Disaster
And treat those two impostors just the same;
If you can bear to hear the truth you've spoken
Twisted by knaves to make a trap for fools,
Or watch the things you gave your life to, broken,
And stoop and build 'em up with worn-out tools:

If you can make one heap of all your winnings
And risk it on one turn of pitch-and-toss,
And lose, and start again at your beginnings,
And never breathe a word about your loss;
If you can force your heart and nerve and sinew
To serve your turn long after they are gone,
And so hold on when there is nothing in you
Except the Will which says to them: 'Hold on!'

If you can talk with crowds and keep your virtue,
Or walk with Kings—nor lose the common touch,
If neither foes nor loving friends can hurt you,
If all men count with you, but none too much;
If you can fill the unforgiving minute
With sixty seconds' worth of distance run,
Yours is the Earth and everything that's in it,
And — which is more — you'll be a Man, my son!

Rudyard Kipling

Notes for **"Recessional"**

* **Recessional** = a hymn sung as the clergy and choir leave church.

* **awful** = deserving of awe or respect

* **Lest** = conjunction preceding (1) something the speaker does not want to happen, (2) something to be guarded against. Here: Let us not forget, let us beware of forgetting.

* **The tumult and the shouting dies; The captains and the kings depart:** = perhaps the noise of the queen's diamond jubilee celebration or the dissolution of the British empire.

* **Thine ancient sacrifice** = the sacrifice of Christ (crucifixion).

* **An humble and a contrite heart** = humility and contriteness will continue after all is gone.

* **pomp of yesterday** = in the future we may see that all our power is gone

* **Gentiles use, Or lesser breeds** = persons not of the higher status of the English

* **heathen heart** = the heart of any Englishman who calls not on God but on guns to secure the Empire.

This poem was written for the Diamond Jubilee of Queen Victoria in 1897. It is a warning to the British people: (1) that it is only through God that the British Empire rules much of the world; (2) that after all the warlords and kingdoms pass away, there will still remain the example of the sacrifice of Christ ("Thine ancient sacrifice"), humble and contrite. The poet then both suggests (3) that all our power may sink like Ninevah and Tyre (powerful ancient cities that were destroyed) and asks God to please spare good England from that fate. Therefore, (4) we should not boast of our power like persons who do not know the laws of God, or (5) put our trust in guns ("the reeking tube") without asking God's help.

"Lest we forget — lest we forget!"

Recessional*

God of our fathers, known of old,
   Lord of our far-flung battle-line,
Beneath whose awful Hand we hold*
   Dominion over palm and pine —
Lord God of Hosts, be with us yet,
Lest we forget — lest we forget!*

The tumult and the shouting dies;
   The Captains and the Kings depart:*
Still stands Thine ancient sacrifice,*
   An humble and a contrite heart.*
Lord God of Hosts, be with us yet,
Lest we forget — lest we forget!

Far-called, our navies melt away;
   On dune and headland sinks the fire:
Lo, all our pomp of yesterday*
   Is one with Nineveh and Tyre!
Judge of the Nations, spare us yet,
Lest we forget — lest we forget!

If, drunk with sight of power, we loose
   Wild tongues that have not Thee in awe,
Such boastings as the Gentiles use,
   Or lesser breeds without the Law — *
Lord God of Hosts, be with us yet,
Lest we forget — lest we forget!

For heathen heart that puts her trust*
   In reeking tube and iron shard,
All valiant dust that builds on dust,
   And guarding, calls not Thee to guard,
For frantic boast and foolish word —
Thy mercy on Thy People, Lord!

                            Rudyard Kipling

Notes for **"The Song of the Wandering Aengus"**

"The Song of Wandering Aengus" was written in 1899 and most people find it hard to understand.

"Aengus" or "Aengus Og" (Aengus the Young) was, according to Irish folklore, the god of love, youth and beauty from the Tuathat de Dannan, a mythical people said to have conquered all of Ireland at one point. Also, in some old myths there is a 'Tree of Life' that has both golden and silver apples, where within the sun and the moon can also symbolize the unity of a man and woman respectively in bringing life into the world.

Using figurative terms of fluctuating light: flickering, fire of flame, glimmering and brightening, Yeats' imagery here suggests just how elusive any 'catch' and/or life-pursuit can be. Is this poem a quest for the glimmering girl who "ran and faded," or is it really for the golden and silver apples? Also, is the poet writing from point of view of a young man on a quest, or from the perspective of an old man?

Many critics believe the "glimmering girl with apple blossom in her hair" to be Maud Gonne, the English-born revolutionary who fought for a nationalist Ireland. Yeats and Gonne had a relationship, and she was an inspiration for many of his poems. But Maud refused Yeats' many marriage proposals, slipping through his hands in pursuit so to speak, and yet his love for her was forever enduring. Does this poem reflect Yeat's endless pursuit of this unrequited love?

The phrase, *"The Golden Apples of the Sun"* was used by the science fiction novelist Ray Bradbury as a title for a collection of his short stories. For a recent musical version of this poem, listen to the song of the same title by American Celtic group Solas on their 2016 release *All These Years*.

William Butler Yeats (1865~1939) was an Irish poet and playwright, considered one of the greatest poets of the twentieth century. He won the Nobel Prize for Literature in 1923. Yeats is best known for his lyrics of imagery, and his most famous poem is "The Second Coming."

"The silver apples of the moon,
The golden apples of the sun."

The Song of the Wandering Aengus

I went out to the hazel wood,
Because a fire was in my head,
And cut and peeled a hazel wand,
And hooked a berry to a thread;
And when white moths were on the wing,
And moth-like stars were flickering out,
I dropped the berry in a stream
And caught a little silver trout.

When I had laid it on the floor
I went to blow the fire a-flame,
But something rustled on the floor,
And some one called me by my name:
It had become a glimmering girl
With apple blossom in her hair
Who called me by my name and ran
And faded through the brightening air.

Though I am old with wandering
Through hollow lands and hilly lands,
I will find out where she has gone,
And kiss her lips and take her hands;
And walk among long dappled grass,
And pluck till time and times are done
The silver apples of the moon,
The golden apples of the sun.

William Butler Yeats

Notes for **"The Second Coming"**

Although widely quoted, "The Second Coming" is not an easy poem to understand. The first stanza of "The Second Coming" describes the poet's view of the present world. Lines from this stanza are quoted often and used as titles of plays, novels and essays. The poet describes a falcon turning in an ever-widening circle, moving farther and farther from the control of the falconer. Is this a metaphor for a failure of a leader to control? Or, does it mean people ('the falcon') are paying less and less attention to the leader? The poet sees that things fall apart, with no center to hold them together - powerless like the falconer - and anarchy reigns. And then he contrasts blood and innocence and what he sees as the attitudes of the best and the worst people.

In the second stanza, the poet concludes that a "Second Coming" is immanent. Obviously it is not the "Second Coming" of Christ arriving in clouds of glory predicted in the Bible; rather the poet sees a *Spiritus Mundi* (spirit of the world) in the form of a "rough beast," a sphinx-like animal rising in the desert and lumbering toward Bethlehem (contrast this image with Shelley's "Ozymandias" in this collection). Writing in 1919, both right after World War I and in the midst of the Russian Revolution, Yeats envisions the cycles of history giving way to a civilization falling apart. The poet intimates that twenty centuries of sleep have been troubled and agitated into a "nightmare by a rocking cradle" (possibly the birth of Jesus), and now — twenty centuries later — "what rough beast, its hour come round at last," appears slouching "toward Bethlehem to be born?" Perhaps the First World War has both "drowned" the "innocence" born twenty centuries previous.

William Butler Yeats (1865~1939) was an Irish poet and playwright, considered one of the greatest poets of the twentieth century, winning the Nobel Prize for Literature in 1923. Yeats is best known for his lyrics, and his most famous poem is "The Second Coming." There are numerous versions of the poem. This is the version published in 1920.

"Things fall apart; the centre cannot hold;...."

**"The best lack all conviction, while the worst
Are full of passionate intensity."**

The Second Coming

Turning and turning in the widening gyre
The falcon cannot hear the falconer;
Things fall apart; the centre cannot hold;
Mere anarchy is loosed upon the world,
The blood-dimmed tide is loosed, and everywhere
The ceremony of innocence is drowned;
The best lack all conviction, while the worst
Are full of passionate intensity.

Surely some revelation is at hand;
Surely the Second Coming is at hand.
The Second Coming! Hardly are those words out
When a vast image out of *Spiritus Mundi*
Troubles my sight: a waste of desert sand;
A shape with lion body and the head of a man,
A gaze blank and pitiless as the sun,
Is moving its slow thighs, while all about it
Wind shadows of the indignant desert birds.
The darkness drops again; but now I know
That twenty centuries of stony sleep
Were vexed to nightmare by a rocking cradle,
And what rough beast, its hour come round at last,
Slouches towards Bethlehem to be born?

William Butler Yeats

Notes for **"Tarantella"**

Written in 1929 and notable for its strong assonance (repetition of vowel sounds), multiple rhymes – both internal as well as line-ending – "Tarantella" harkens back to a meeting Joseph Hilaire Belloc had with Miranda Mackintosh (a Scottish citizen) twenty years earlier at an inn in the Pyrenean hamlet of Canfranc along the Aragon River.

Mimicking the movement, sounds and rhythm of the Spanish (Pyrenean) dance called the *Tarantella* performed during his stay, Belloc's first stanza recalls his initial, lively, light-hearted and entertaining visit to the inn in 1909. Towards the end of the first stanza, however, the poet begins transitioning from past to present, using the dancers' "Out and in--" movements to signal both how all the 'ins' of the Inn will be 'out' and how the 'outs' have come *in*to the Inn — altogether now just a memory twenty years later.

Perhaps reflecting the economic decline in Spain that accompanied its monarchy becoming a republican state in 1929, the final stanza's heavy movements, sounds and rhythms from the outside environment are now the empty 'ins' of the Inn, absent the merriment of sounds of feet now "dead to the ground" — that "never more" will tread. The poet further emphasizes the present emptiness within the "walls of the halls" of the Inn by bringing in the outside, echoed "boom" of the Aragon River's distant waterfall.

How are the words "Miranda" and "remember" and "Never more" alike? And how is this poem and Edgar Allen Poe's "The Raven" similar in sound(s), rhythm and rhyme?

Joseph Hilaire Belloc (July 7, 1870~July 16, 1953) was an Anglo-French writer and historian who became a naturalized British subject in 1902. He was one of the most prolific writers in England during the early twentieth century. His Catholic faith infused much of his writing, and he often collaborated with the essayist and novelist G. K. Chesterton.

"Do you remember an Inn, Miranda?"
Tarantella

Do you remember an Inn,
Miranda?
Do you remember an Inn?
And the tedding and the spreading
Of the straw for a bedding,
And the fleas that tease in the High Pyrenees,
And the wine that tasted of tar?
And the cheers and the jeers of the young muleteers
(Under the vine of the dark veranda)?
Do you remember an Inn, Miranda,
Do you remember an Inn?
And the cheers and the jeers of the young muleteers
Who hadn't got a penny,
And who weren't paying any,
And the hammer at the doors and the din?
And the hip! hop! hap!
Of the clap
Of the hands to the swirl and the twirl
Of the girl gone chancing,
Glancing,
Dancing,
Backing and advancing,
Snapping of the clapper to the spin
Out and in —
And the ting, tong, tang of the guitar!
Do you remember an Inn,
Miranda?
Do you remember an Inn?
  Never more;
  Miranda,
  Never more.
  Only the high peaks hoar;
  And Aragon a torrent at the door.
  No sound
  In the walls of the halls where falls
  The tread
  Of the feet of the dead to the ground,
  No sound:
  But the boom
  Of the far waterfall like doom. *Joseph Hilaire Belloc*

Notes for **"Sympathy"**

In this poem a bird throws itself against the bars of its cage trying to become free. The bird bleeds and has to stop, but then it tries again. Its song is a prayer for freedom.

The contemporary poet, Maya Angelou (1923-2014) used Dunbar's last line: "I know why the caged bird sings!" as both the title of her hugely successful, early memoirs in 1969 and later in 1983 when she published a poem entitled "Caged Bird."

The poem's theme is not so different from the seamstress in Thomas Hood's "The Song of the Shirt" written in 1843, or of William Blake's "The Chimney Sweeper: My Mother Died When I Was Very Young." The 'caged bird,' seamstress and chimney sweep all seek liberation or freedom in a world beyond their particular imprisonment.

Paul Laurence Dunbar (1872~1906) was a poet, short story writer, novelist and editor. He was the son of a slave, wrote on African American themes, and was a great influence on later poets. Two years before he graduated from high school Dunbar published poems in the *Dayton Herald*. He also worked as an editor of the *Dayton Tattler*, a newspaper for African Americans published by Orville Wright (who later worked with his brother Wilbur inventing the airplane). In 1893, at the age of twenty-one, Dunbar published his first poem collection and thereafter had poems published in *Harpers* and *The New York Times*. Later he made a successful reading tour in England. Returning to the U.S., he worked as an elevator operator and then as clerk at the Library of Congress.

He continued to publish until shortly before his death in 1906.

"I know why the caged bird sings!"

Sympathy

I know what the caged bird feels, alas!
When the sun is bright on the upland slopes;
When the wind stirs soft through the springing grass,
And the river flows like a stream of glass;
When the first bird sings and the first bud opes,
And the faint perfume from its chalice steals —
I know what the caged bird feels!

I know why the caged bird beats his wing
Till its blood is red on the cruel bars;
For he must fly back to his perch and cling
When he fain would be on the bough a-swing;
And a pain still throbs in the old, old scars
And they pulse again with a keener sting —
I know why he beats his wing!

I know why the caged bird sings, ah me,
When his wing is bruised and his bosom sore, —
When he beats his bars and he would be free;
It is not a carol of joy or glee,
But a prayer that he sends from his heart's deep core,
But a plea, that upward to Heaven he flings —
I know why the caged bird sings!

Paul Laurence Dunbar

Notes for **"We Wear the Mask"**

This poem can refer to a universal human situation, but when the reader realizes an African Amerian wrote this poem in the late 1890s, it becomes poignant and tragic given the conditions of the African American at the time.

Indeed, the famous American playwright Eugene O'Neill may have picked-up on both Dunbar's poem here and not only the psychological plight of the enslaved African American but also all people when he once stated in an *American Spectator* interview: "One's outer life passes in a solitude haunted by the masks of others; one's inner life passes in a solitude hounded by the masks of oneself."

The poem is a *rondeau* (similar to John McCrae's "In Flanders Fields"), that displays the author's mastery of the classical form. A *rondeau* (French for 'round') is a fifteen-line poem, with the opening words being used twice as a refrain and using only two, end-rhyme schemes throughout the poem. Commonly set to music between the 13th and 15th centuries, the *rondeau*, along with the *ballade* and the *virelai* was one of the three French verse forms popular at the time.

Paul Lawrence Dunbar (1872~1906) was a poet, short story writer, novelist and editor. He was the son of a slave, wrote on African American themes, and was a great influence on later poets.

"We wear the mask!"

We Wear the Mask

We wear the mask that grins and lies,
It hides our cheeks and shades our eyes, —
This debt we pay to human guile;
With torn and bleeding hearts we smile,
And mouth with myriad subtleties.

Why should the world be over-wise,
In counting all our tears and sighs?
Nay, let them only see us, while
    We wear the mask.

We smile, but, O great Christ, our cries
To thee from tortured souls arise.
We sing, but oh the clay is vile
Beneath our feet, and long the mile;
But let the world dream otherwise,
    We wear the mask!

Paul Laurence Dunbar

Notes for **"The Listeners"**

Many people have attempted to figure-out what this poem is all about. A wonderful symmetry of sound-to-silence both starts and finishes the poem, as the reader is brought into an eerie world of silence punctuated by a first knocking; then not just one heavier "smote" but yet another, and an "even louder" subsequent smote on the door before the Traveller departs. And yet the reader's curiosity is drawn deeply into a silence that becomes alive.

Note how de la Mare keeps the poem in motion using "-ing" forms and end rhyme, so that, although the Traveller has dismounted and the house is supposedly empty with no apparent reply to his overtures, there is nonetheless movement outside and within the house's seemingly still architecture. Note further the movement of the animals in the poem: the Traveller's horse; the bird. "The Listeners" hear and have heard the voice, yet why are they not answering?

What is happening and why? Did the Traveler once live there? Was the Traveler sent by "them"? Could this poem be about keeping one's word even when there is no one around to appreciate keeping one's word?

And did de la Mare keep his word to you, the reader? In the strange architecture of your own mind, did you find yourself listening for the answer to the Traveller's entreaties? Read the poem again slowly, and catch just how closely you find yourself listening for a response to the Traveller's increasingly anxious knocking and cries. Are you not soon within the "lone house" yourself, listening?

Might Walter de la Mare be suggesting that the reader of this poem be the "Listener;" one who must be attentive to the inquiries and awakenings of others yet also content sometimes with only the seemingly unsatisfactory answer of 'stillness'? What is *your* answer?

"Is there anybody there?"

The Listeners

'Is there anybody there?' said the Traveller,
   Knocking on the moonlit door;
And his horse in the silence champed the grasses
    Of the forest's ferny floor:
And a bird flew up out of the turret,
   Above the Traveller's head:
And he smote upon the door again a second time;
   'Is there anybody there?' he said.

But no one descended to the Traveller;
   No head from the leaf-fringed sill
Leaned over and looked into his grey eyes,
   Where he stood perplexed and still.
But only a host of phantom listeners
  That dwelt in the lone house then
Stood listening in the quiet of the moonlight
  To that voice from the world of men:
Stood thronging the faint moonbeams on the dark stair,
  That goes down to the empty hall,
Hearkening in an air stirred and shaken
  By the lonely Traveller's call.

Notes for **"The Listeners"** (cont.)

Walter de la Mare (1873~1956) was an English poet, short story writer, and novelist. He wrote about childhood, nature, dreams, death, rare states of mind and the uncanny. "The Listeners" is one of his most famous and haunting poems, and as he has exhibited in this poem, de la Mare was known as a master in manipulating poetical structures.

And he felt in his heart their strangeness,
  Their stillness answering his cry,
While his horse moved, cropping the dark turf,
  'Neath the starred and leafy sky;
For he suddenly smote on the door, even
  Louder, and lifted his head: —
'Tell them I came, and no one answered,
  That I kept my word,' he said.
Never the least stir made the listeners,
  Though every word he spake
Fell echoing through the shadowiness of the still
house
  From the one man left awake:
Ay, they heard his foot upon the stirrup,
  And the sound of iron on stone,
And how the silence surged softly backward,
  When the plunging hoofs were gone.

Walter de la Mare

Notes for **"Mending Wall"**

"Mending Wall" is about a poet and his neighbor, who periodically walk together to repair the breaks in the stone wall that separates their properties. The poet wonders why there is a need for walls. Seeing that the forces of nature occasionally cause the wall to fall down, he thinks, "Something there is that doesn't love a wall." He also thinks, before he himself built a wall, he'd want to know what he was walling in and walling out. But the neighbor, whom the poet describes as bringing stones as "an old-stone savage armed" and moving in darkness, just repeats his father's saying, "Good fences make good neighbours." The poem also implies a friendly but detached relationship between the neighbors.

Some people suggest that the line "Good fences make good neighbours" to be Frost's view of life, but that phrase comes from the neighbor, who unquestionably received it from his father. As the poem shows, Frost's view is quite the opposite. The poet may even regard his neighbor as a bit retrograde.

And yet, some people assert that good relationships, even the most intimate, flourish best when each person consciously protects the solitude of the other. What do you think?

"Something there is that doesn't love a wall,...."
"Good fences make good neighbours."

Mending Wall

Something there is that doesn't love a wall,
That sends the frozen-ground-swell under it,
And spills the upper boulders in the sun;
And makes gaps even two can pass abreast.
The work of hunters is another thing:
I have come after them and made repair
Where they have left not one stone on a stone,
But they would have the rabbit out of hiding,
To please the yelping dogs. The gaps I mean,
No one has seen them made or heard them made,
But at spring mending-time we find them there.
I let my neighbour know beyond the hill;
And on a day we meet to walk the line
And set the wall between us once again.
We keep the wall between us as we go.
To each the boulders that have fallen to each.
And some are loaves and some so nearly balls
We have to use a spell to make them balance:
"Stay where you are until our backs are turned!"
We wear our fingers rough with handling them.
Oh, just another kind of out-door game,
One on a side. It comes to little more:
There where it is we do not need the wall:
He is all pine and I am apple orchard.
My apple trees will never get across
And eat the cones under his pines, I tell him.
He only says, "Good fences make good neighbours."

Notes for **"Mending Wall"** (cont.)

Robert Frost (1874~1963) was a very popular New England Poet, who did not follow the innovations of Walt Whitman but instead wrote in traditional forms that caught the spirit and language of New England. His most famous poems are "Stopping by the Woods on a Snowy Evening," "The Road Not Taken," "Mending Wall," and "The Death of the Hired Man." He won four Pulitzer Prizes for Poetry and read his poem "The Gift Outright" at the inauguration of President John F. Kennedy in 1961.

Spring is the mischief in me, and I wonder
If I could put a notion in his head:
"Why do they make good neighbours? Isn't it
Where there are cows? But here there are no cows.
Before I built a wall I'd ask to know
What I was walling in or walling out,
And to whom I was like to give offence.
Something there is that doesn't love a wall,
That wants it down." I could say "Elves" to him,
But it's not elves exactly, and I'd rather
He said it for himself. I see him there
Bringing a stone grasped firmly by the top
In each hand, like an old-stone savage armed.
He moves in darkness as it seems to me,
Not of woods only and the shade of trees.
He will not go behind his father's saying,
And he likes having thought of it so well
He says again, "Good fences make good neighbours."

Robert Frost

Notes for
"Stopping by Woods on a Snowy Evening"

The poem describes the thoughts of a rider who pauses at night to watch snow falling in the woods. The rider's horse "thinks it queer/ to stop without a farmhouse near." The horse knows that the journey usually stops at a farmhouse; not knowing the rider has stopped to simply to appreciate beauty. The poem ends with the rider reminding himself, in an oft-quoted line, that, despite the beauty of the view, "I have promises to keep / And miles to go before I sleep."

This is one of the most famous short poems in the English language. It is said Jawaharlal Nehru, the first prime minister of independent India, had copied the last stanza of the poem in his own hand and always kept it by his side.

Those lines (if not the whole poem) are worthy of being memorized.

This poem is written in iambic tetrameter, that is, an iambic measure (short syllable - long syllable as in - *da dum*) and four measures (tetra = four; meter = measure) to a line. Therefore,

    "Whose woods these are   I think   I know." =
      da   dum,   da   dum, da dum,   da dum

See Lord Byron's "She Walks in Beauty" in this collection for another example of iambic tetrameter.

Robert Frost (1874~1963) was an American poet who briefly attended Dartmouth and Harvard and then farmed in New England. Poetry was his main vocation. His best-known poems are "Mending Wall," "Death of the Hired Man," "The Road Not Taken," and "Stopping by the Woods on a Snowy Evening." He was a clear-writing, simple poet who used traditional poem forms. At the Inauguration of President John F. Kennedy in 1963 he read his poem "The Gift Outright." He won four Pulitzer Prizes for poetry.

**"...I have promises to keep,
And miles to go before I sleep,
And miles to go before I sleep."**

Stopping by Woods on a Snowy Evening

Whose woods these are I think I know.
His house is in the village though;
He will not see me stopping here
To watch his woods fill up with snow.

My little horse must think it queer
To stop without a farmhouse near
Between the woods and frozen lake
The darkest evening of the year.

He gives his harness bells a shake
To ask if there is some mistake.
The only other sound's the sweep
Of easy wind and downy flake.

The woods are lovely, dark and deep,
But I have promises to keep,
And miles to go before I sleep,
And miles to go before I sleep.

Robert Frost

Notes for **"The Road Not Taken"**

The poet is writing about decisions that a person always has to make in life. Both roads, "one" and "the other," appear to be equally attractive. He took "the other" although it was "really about the same." What does the poet mean when he says "knowing how way leads on to way, I doubted if I should ever come back."? Does this agree with your experience? Do you think the poet's "sigh" is a sigh of satisfaction or a sigh of regret?

Robert Frost (1874~1963) was a very popular New England Poet, who did not follow the innovations of Walt Whitman but instead wrote in traditional forms that caught the spirit and language of New England.

**"...I took the one less travelled by
And that has made all the difference."**

The Road Not Taken

Two roads diverged in a yellow wood,
And sorry I could not travel both
And be one traveler, long I stood
And looked down one as far as I could
To where it bent in the undergrowth;

Then took the other, as just as fair,
And having perhaps the better claim,
Because it was grassy and wanted wear;
Though as for that the passing there
Had worn them really about the same,

And both that morning equally lay
In leaves no step had trodden black.
Oh, I kept the first for another day!
Yet knowing how way leads on to way,
I doubted if I should ever come back.

I shall be telling this with a sigh
Somewhere ages and ages hence:
Two roads diverged in a wood, and I —
I took the one less traveled by,
And that has made all the difference.

Robert Frost

Notes for **"Sea Fever"**

Repeating a "call" that "cannot be denied" three times, the poet here is continually pulled to thrills and adventures at sea. Both invoking a mood of freedom through the imagery sea gulls, whales and traveling gypsies – and appealing to the reader's senses of sight, sound and touch, the poet explains the 'feverish' lure of ocean adventures, perhaps additionally "turning a trick" in comparing life to a sea voyage, a quiet sleep and sweet dreams when it's over. Another meaning for "trick" is its nautical nuance of 'taking a turn at the ship's wheel,' and perhaps Masefield, who began his seafaring ways at age fifteen, in this poem relates how life resembles a personal, destined voyage through which one steers her/his own vessel, needing only a "star" as a compass for our chosen journeys. An earlier work in this collection, "Invictus" (p. 233), echoes Masefield's "call": "I am the master of my fate, I am the captain of my soul," and Masefield's "And quiet sleep and a sweet dream when the long trick's over" can be said to even harken back to Hamlet's Act 3; Scene 1 line: "To die, to sleep–To sleep– perchance to dream" (p. 39 in this collection as well).

This poem is meant to be read or performed aloud, and a great, YouTube recitation to access the rolling-waves' rhythm of this selection can be found by 'googling' its title. Not only does Masefield use the two-syllable, da-DUM "iambic" heartbeat, but he also mixes dactyls: DUM da da (cf. p. 192 first paragraph in this collection) and seven-'foot,' four-by-three (heptameter) spondees, along with alliteration (cf. p. 2 [bottom] and p. 168 [top]), to mimic the rhythm of rolling waves. Watch the YouTube recitation of this poem, read the poem aloud to yourself, and see if you can catch the cadence of the waves in your own ship's "voyage"!

John Masefield, (1878~1967) a novelist and poet, was the English Poet Laureate from 1930 until he died in 1967. He wrote many poems about the sea collected in *Salt-Water Poems and Ballads*. This poem was written in 1902. The Poet Laureate is the official poet of a country; in England a post appointed by the King or Queen. The Poet Laureate's duties are to write a poem on the monarch's birthday and on special occasions for the country.

**"…all I ask is a tall ship
and a star to steer her by;.…"**

Sea Fever

I must go down to the seas again,
               to the lonely sea and the sky,
And all I ask is a tall ship
               and a star to steer her by;
And the wheel's kick and the wind's song
               and the white sail's shaking,
And a grey mist on the sea's face,
               and a grey dawn breaking.

I must go down to the seas again,
               for the call of the running tide
Is a wild call and a clear call
               that may not be denied;
And all I ask is a windy day
               with the white clouds flying,
And the flung spray and the blown spume,
               and the sea-gulls crying.

I must go down to the seas again,
               to the vagrant gypsy life,
To the gull's way and the whale's way
               where the wind's like a whetted knife;
And all I ask is a merry yarn
               from a laughing fellow-rover,
And quiet sleep and a sweet dream
               when the long trick's over.

John Masefield

Notes for **"Chicago"**

Carl Sandburg wrote the poem "Chicago" in 1914. In this, one of his most famous poems, Sandburg illuminates the pride, youth and vigor of Chicago and its people despite the city's darker aspects and shortcomings. Chicago at this point is both the "freight handler to the nation" and the world and domestic trade-hub of America, a city through which so much vital industry passes. Sandburg's use of the "–ing" verse-form throughout the poem keeps pace with both the industriousness of Chicago and its active citizenry, who laugh and work in sometimes brutal conditions, "…piling job upon job…."

Carl Sandburg (1878~1967) Poet, writer, folklorist; born in Galesburg, Illinois, he worked as an editor, journalist, copywriter, lecturer, and collector of folk songs. Sandburg won the Pulitzer Prize (1940) for the last of his six-volume biography of Abraham Lincoln (1926~1939). He was deeply interested in American folksong and lore, collected some 300 folksongs and ballads in *The American Songbag* (1927), and he often gave public recitals, accompanying himself on the guitar. He also wrote children's books and a novel *Remembrance Rock* (1948). Although he lived in Chicago for much of his life, he later retired to Flat Rock, N.C where he died in 1967.

CARL SANDBURG

"City of the Big Shoulders"
"Freight Handler to the Nation."

Chicago

Hog Butcher to the World,
   Tool Maker, Stacker of Wheat,
   Player with Railroads and the Nation's Freight Handler;
   Stormy, husky, brawling,
   City of the Big Shoulders:

They tell me you are wicked and I believe them,
   for I have seen your painted women
   under the gas lamps luring the farm boys.
And they tell me you are crooked and I answer: Yes,
   it is true I have seen the gunmen kill and go free
   to kill again.
And they tell me you are brutal and my reply is:
   On the faces of women and children I have seen
   the marks of wanton hunger.
And having answered so I turn once more to those
   who sneer at this my city,
   and I give them back the sneer and say to them:
Come and show me another city with lifted head
   singing so proud to be alive and coarse and strong
   and cunning.
Flinging magnetic curses amid the toil of piling
   job upon job, here is a tall bold slugger set vivid
   against little soft cities;
Fierce as a dog with tongue lapping for action,
   cunning as a savage pitted against the wilderness,
   Bareheaded,
   Shoveling,
   Wrecking,
   Planning,
   Building, breaking, rebuilding,

Under the smoke, dust all over his mouth,
laughing with white teeth,
Under the terrible burden of destiny
laughing as a young man laughs,
Laughing even as an ignorant fighter laughs
who has never lost a battle,
Bragging and laughing that under his wrist is the pulse,
and under his ribs the heart of the people,
    Laughing!
Laughing the stormy, husky, brawling laughter of Youth,
half-naked, sweating to be proud to be
    Hog Butcher,
    Tool Maker,
    Stacker of Wheat,
    Player with Railroads and
    Freight Handler to the Nation.

Carl Sandburg

Notes for **"Fog"**

The poem "Fog" contains a very famous use of metaphor (a metaphor is when we compare one thing [here -the fog] with another [here -a cat] without saying "the fog is <u>like</u> a cat." For example, often to show that persons can be brought to justice, we might refer to "the long arm of the law" even though the law does not have arms. Other examples would include "a blanket of snow" or "keep your eyes peeled" or "the crack of dawn."

Here, to give the reader a feeling for fog, the poet compares the weather to the stealthy movement, posture, and silence of a cat. Literally, Sandburg's cat imagery allows us to imagine the "fog" as well. Obviously, a comparison with a dog would not do, would it?

For a more extensive explanation of metaphor, see Henry Wadsworth Longfellow's "The Landlord's Tale. Paul Revere's Ride" in this collection.

This poem, "Fog" (1916) and "Chicago" (1914) are two of Carl Sandburg's best-known poems.

Carl Sandburg (1878~1967) Poet, writer, folklorist; born in Galesburg, Illinois, he worked as an editor, journalist, copywriter, lecturer, and collector of folk songs.

**"The fog comes
on little cat feet."**

Fog

The fog comes
on little cat feet.
It sits looking
over harbor and city
on silent haunches
and then moves on.

Carl Sandburg

Notes for **"The Grass"**

This poem is about people, history and nature. It is narrated by the "grass" which, as part of nature, has to do its work.

"The grass" observes people who continually war with one another. Austerlitz and Waterloo were places of great battles in the wars of Napoleon; Gettysburg was the great battle of the U.S. Civil War; Ypres and Verdun were battles in World War I. The poem suggests memories of these great tragedies are and will be forgotten as time passes when the grass covers the graves. Soon train passengers will not even recognize that so many people lost their lives in these places. The implication is that wars will go on and nature and time will cause people to forget. "Let me work" also implies that nature will eventually undo what humans have done.

This poem, in fact the entire poem, is an example of the literary device called *personification*, which refers to the practice of attaching and/or attributing human traits and characteristics to supposedly inanimate objects, events, and animals. See "The Landlord's Tale. Paul Revere's Ride" (pages 154–161 in this collection) for both further explanation and other examples of personification.

Contained in a 103-poem collection entitled *Cornhuskers*, this poem was first published in New York in 1918, shortly after World War I. Sandburg foresaw that the great carnage of that war would soon be forgotten, as indeed it was.

Carl Sandburg (1878~1967) Poet, writer, folklorist; born in Galesburg, Illinois, he worked as an editor, journalist, copywriter, lecturer, and collector of folk songs.

**"I am the grass.
Let me work."**

The Grass

Pile the bodies high at Austerlitz and Waterloo.
Shovel them under and let me work —
I am the grass; I cover all.

And pile them high at Gettysburg
And pile them high at Ypres and Verdun.
Shovel them under and let me work.
Two years, ten years, and the passengers ask the
conductor: *
What place is this?
Where are we now?

I am the grass.
Let me work.

Carl Sandburg

* **conductor** = train attendant, trainmaster,
or train-car cabin attendant

Notes for **"In Flanders Fields"**

After burying his friend Lieutenant Alexis Helmern, who was killed during the Second Battle of Ypres in Belgium in World War I, Canadian army physician John McCrae wrote this poem in May, 1915. The battle was fought outside Ypres in Flanders Field, a field full of poppies. Because certain strains of poppies produce opium, poppies are often considered both a potent painkiller and a symbol of sleep. The poem became very popular and led to the poppy being adopted as a symbol of remembrance of World War I, which was then thought to be "…the war to end all wars." The poem shows McCrae's strong belief in the cause for which he was fighting.

The poem is a *rondeau* (French for 'round'), a classical thirteenth century, fifteen-line, French poetic form with a *rentrement* (the first few words of the first line of the first stanza are repeated as the last line of both the second and third stanzas). The *rondeau* rhyme scheme is (**aabba – aabR – aabbaR**).

McCrae submitted the poem to *Punch* magazine, which published it late in 1915. The editors of *Punch* changed the last word of line one from "grow" to "blow" for the reason that "grow" was used in line fourteen.

John McCrae (1872~1918), an army doctor, who was also a poet and artist, was born in Canada. He was a prolific writer, wrote a daily diary, published several short stories, and wrote more than forty medical articles. In 1914 he served as a field surgeon in the Canadian Field Artillery. He died from pneumonia and meningitis in a hospital in France in January 1918.

"In Flanders fields the poppies blow...."

In Flanders Fields

In Flanders fields the poppies blow
Between the crosses, row on row,
   That mark our place; and in the sky
   The larks, still bravely singing, fly
Scarce heard amid the guns below.

We are the Dead. Short days ago
We lived, felt dawn, saw sunset glow,
   Loved and were loved, and now we lie,
     In Flanders fields.

Take up our quarrel with the foe:
To you from failing hands we throw
   The torch; be yours to hold it high.
   If ye break faith with us who die
We shall not sleep, though poppies grow
     In Flanders fields.

John McCrae

Notes for **"Trees"**

Although the poem "Trees" has been the subject of many parodies and criticized as being too simple and full of mixed metaphors (the tree's mouth is pressed against the earth, while it looks at the sky, and its leafy arms are the same as its hair and its bosom), it is, nevertheless, said to be the one poem known by practically everybody. Note how Kilmer first builds his tree from bottom to top and then describes its contents.

Both Rutgers, where Kilmer spent two years before transferring to Columbia, and Notre Dame, where Kilmer gave some lectures on writing, claim the tree that inspired his poem.

Notre Dame bases its claim on a statement by a personal friend of Kilmer, the Reverend Charles O'Donnell, C.S.C, who at one time was the Poet Laureate of Indiana and from 1928 to 1934 the President of the University of Notre Dame, that "The big tree that shades Our Lady's niche at the Notre Dame Grotto; 'a tree that looks at God all day and lifts her leafy arms to pray,' was the inspiration for Kilmer's poem." It is also said that the stump of that tree is still visible today.

(Alfred) Joyce Kilmer (1886~1918) was an American poet remembered mostly for the poem "Trees" written in 1913. Kilmer's poetry was influenced by his strong religious faith and his dedication to the natural beauty of the world. During the First World War Kilmer voluntarily enlisted and served in the 69th Infantry Regiment ("The Fighting 69th" also known as "The Fighting Irish Brigade"). At the age of thirty-one, he was killed in the Second Battle of the Marne on July 30, 1918.

"...only God can make a tree."

Trees

I think that I shall never see
A poem lovely as a tree.

A tree whose hungry mouth is prest
Against the sweet earth's flowing breast;

A tree that looks at God all day,
And lifts her leafy arms to pray;

A tree that may in summer wear
A nest of robins in her hair;

Upon whose bosom snow has lain;
Who intimately lives with rain.

Poems are made by fools like me,
But only God can make a tree.

Joyce Kilmer

Notes for **"I Have a Rendezvous with Death"**

This poem reflects both Alan Seeger's belief in the justness of World War I and in his recognition that many who enlisted to fight would not survive. From first to last stanza, this premonition about his own rendezvous with death intensifies in each stanza of the poem: "disputed barricade" to "battered hill" to "flaming town." Although death may "pass him still," as suggested in the second stanza, and it would be more pleasant to be comfortable at home, as the third stanza further suggests, the poet will remain true to his pledge and soon be off to make the rendezvous.

This poem is written mostly in iambic (unstressed-stressed; *da dum da dum da dum da dum*) feet: tetrameter (four "feet" [*da dum*] to a line).

Alan Seeger was the uncle of the recently deceased folk singer Pete Seeger. When one juxtaposes each stanza's reference to the coming of spring in this poem and its "first-meadow flowers," Pete Seeger's song entitled "Where Have All the Flowers Gone" — another anthem to the inevitable casualties of war — easily comes to mind. You can search Pete Seeger's lyrics on the internet to discover the uncanny lyrical connection between the relatives.

Alan Seeger (June 22, 1888~July 4, 1916) was an American poet who fought in World War I. Before the United States entered the war, Seeger, who was living in London after graduating from Harvard, joined the French Foreign Legion and died while fighting with them during the Battle of the Somme. His best known poem is "I Have a Rendezvous with Death."

"I have a rendezvous with Death...."

I Have a Rendezvous with Death

I have a rendezvous with Death
At some disputed barricade,
When Spring comes back with rustling shade
And apple-blossoms fill the air —
I have a rendezvous with Death
When Spring brings back blue days and fair.

It may be he shall take my hand
And lead me into his dark land
And close my eyes and quench my breath —
It may be I shall pass him still.
I have a rendezvous with Death
On some scarred slope of battered hill,
When Spring comes round again this year
And the first meadow-flowers appear.

God knows 'twere better to be deep
Pillowed in silk and scented down,
Where love throbs out in blissful sleep,
Pulse nigh to pulse, and breath to breath,
Where hushed awakenings are dear...
But I've a rendezvous with Death
At midnight in some flaming town,
When Spring trips north again this year,
And I to my pledged word am true,
I shall not fail that rendezvous.

Alan Seeger

Notes for **"Burnt Norton"**

This is 'Section One' of five sections of T.S. Eliot's poem "Burnt Norton," which in its entirety is a meditation on time and religion. Written in 1935, "Burnt Norton" is the first of four poems in Eliot's "Four Quartets."

Among the factors that may have influenced this first of the five sections is that Burnt Norton is the name of a manor house with gardens in Gloucestershire, England that Eliot visited in 1934. The house had a rose garden with a path to an empty pool.

In addition, Eliot is said to have been influenced by Albert Einstein's 1905 publication of *Specialized and General Theories of Relativity*, concerning the relationship between time and space and postulating, among other things, that there is little distinction between the past, present and future; that time is relative to the place of the observer.

Also, a chemist friend has suggested that Eliot may have been influenced by both Werner Heisenberg's 1929 uncertainty principle, which states that motion and position each can be measured, but not both simultaneously, and the "observer effect," that is, the very act of measurement, affects the object being measured (e.g. think of observing with an electron microscope). So: "...the roses/ Had the look of flowers that are looked at."

"...human kind cannot bear very much reality."

Burnt Norton
(Part I of the first of Eliot's *The Four Quartets*)

Time present and time past
Are both perhaps present in time future
And time future contained in time past.
If all time is eternally present
All time is unredeemable.
What might have been is an abstraction
Remaining a perpetual possibility
Only in a world of speculation.
What might have been and what has been
Point to one end, which is always present.
Footfalls echo in the memory
Down the passage which we did not take
Towards the door we never opened
Into the rose-garden. My words echo
Thus, in your mind.
      But to what purpose
Disturbing the dust on a bowl of rose-leaves
I do not know.
      Other echoes
Inhabit the garden. Shall we follow?
Quick, said the bird, find them, find them,
Round the corner. Through the first gate,
Into our first world, shall we follow
The deception of the thrush? Into our first world.
There they were, dignified, invisible,
Moving without pressure, over the dead leaves,
In the autumn heat, through the vibrant air,
And the bird called, in response to
The unheard music hidden in the shrubbery,
And the unseen eyebeam crossed, for the roses
Had the look of flowers that are looked at.

Notes for **"Burnt Norton"** (cont.)

In part five of "Burnt Norton" (not printed here), Eliot, himself, realizes that these concepts are difficult to express saying in part:

"....Words strain,
Crack and sometimes break, under the burden,
Under the tension, slip, slide, perish,
Decay with imprecision, will not stay in place,
Will not stay still."

Surely, you have had that experience.

The line, "...human kind cannot bear very much reality," also appeared in Part III of Eliot's 1935 play *Murder in the Cathedral*, which is about the assassination of Thomas a'Becket in the cathedral at Canterbury.

T.S. Eliot (Thomas Sterns Eliot) (1888~1965), a playwright, critic, and one of the major poets of the twentieth century, was born in St. Louis, Missouri. After studying philosophy at Harvard, at age twenty-five he moved to England and eventually became a British citizen. He converted to the Anglican faith in 1927. His major poems were "The Love Song of J. Alfred Prufrock" (1915), "The Waste Land" (1922), "The Hollow Men" (1925), "Ash Wednesday" (1930) and "The Four Quartets" (four poems published together in 1942). He was awarded the Nobel Prize for Literature in 1948.

There they were as our guests, accepted and accepting.
So we moved, and they, in a formal pattern,
Along the empty alley, into the box circle,
To look down into the drained pool.
Dry the pool, dry concrete, brown edged,
And the pool was filled with water out of sunlight,
And the lotos rose, quietly, quietly,
The surface glittered out of heart of light,
And they were behind us, reflected in the pool.
Then a cloud passed, and the pool was empty.
Go, said the bird, for the leaves were full of children,
Hidden excitedly, containing laughter.
Go, go, go, said the bird: human kind
Cannot bear very much reality.
Time past and time future
What might have been and what has been
Point to one end, which is always present.

T.S. Eliot

Notes for **"Choruses from The Rock"**

These lines are the opening lines of a long dramatic reading called "The Rock." In these verses the poet reflects on the continual motion of animals and people, the universe and the seasons, and suggests that, as a result, we have knowledge of motion, but not of stillness or silence. The "Word" here no doubt refers to God.

Often quoted are the lines about "where is the wisdom we have lost in knowledge" and "where is the knowledge we have lost in information."

What are the differences between information, knowledge and wisdom?

Perhaps with all the information available today these lines are even more pertinent than when the poet wrote them in 1934 before there was any internet or even television. We are now overwhelmed with all the information of movement and sound that has crowded out stillness and silence. The poet asks whether this ongoing tendency brings us any closer to God.

A interesting exercise might be to reread William Butler Yeats' "The Second Coming" on page 267 in this collection, compare and contrast Yeats' and Eliot's themes and imagery, and then finally consider what you think Yeats and Eliot were responding to in writing these verses.

T.S. Eliot (Thomas Stearns Eliot) (1888~1965) was an American-born English poet, critic and dramatist who lived in England after 1914. He is considered one of the major poets of the twentieth century. Trying to use the natural rhythms of speech, T.S. Eliot wrote about society and religion. His famous poems, "The Love Song of J. Alfred Prufrock" (1919) and "The Waste Land" (1922) are about the spiritual emptiness of the modern world. Another is "The Four Quartets," which is about time and space and man's desire to be free of them. His famous plays are *The Cocktail Party* and *Murder in the Cathedral* (about the death of Thomas a'Becket). And for fun he wrote *The Old Possum's Book of Practical Cats*, which Andrew Lloyd Weber used as the basis for the Broadway musical *Cats*.

"Where is the life we have lost in living?"

"Where is the wisdom we have lost in knowledge?"

"Where is the knowledge we have lost in information?"

Choruses from The Rock
(opening lines)

The Eagle soars in the summit of Heaven,
The Hunter with his dogs pursues his circuit.
O perpetual revolution of configured stars,
O perpetual recurrence of determined seasons,
O world of spring and autumn, birth and dying!

The endless cycle of idea and action,
Endless invention, endless experiment,
Brings knowledge of motion, but not of stillness;
Knowledge of speech, but not of silence;
Knowledge of words, and ignorance of the Word.

All our knowledge brings us nearer to death,
But nearness to death no nearer to God.
Where is the Life we have lost in living?
Where is the wisdom we have lost in knowledge?
Where is the knowledge we have lost in information?

The cycles of Heaven in twenty centuries
Brings us farther from God and nearer to the Dust.

T.S. Eliot

Notes for **"The Hollow Men"**

"The Hollow Men" was published in 1925 and reflects the poet's belief in the cultural and spiritual emptiness of the beginning of the twentieth century. The poem combines fragments of commentary, children's rhymes, liturgy, and ends with some of the most quoted lines of the twentieth century. The two epigraphs "Mistah Kurtz-he dead," refer to Joseph Conrad's *Heart of Darkness* and "A penny for the Old Guy" to a children's game about a stuffed effigy (hollow) of Guy Fawkes. Some scholars believe that the term "hollow men" comes from the play *Julius Caesar* Act 4; Scene 2, where Brutus is commenting on the recent change of attitude of Cassius, his fellow general.

"This is the way the world ends
Not with a bang but a whimper."

The Hollow Men
(excerpts)
***** = omitted lines

Mistah Kurtz-he dead
A penny for the Old Guy

I

We are the hollow men
We are the stuffed men
Leaning together
Headpiece filled with straw. Alas!
Our dried voices, when
We whisper together
Are quiet and meaningless
As wind in dry grass
Or rats' feet over broken glass
In our dry cellar

Shape without form, shade without colour,
Paralysed force, gesture without motion;

Those who have crossed
With direct eyes, to death's other Kingdom
Remember us-if at all-not as lost
Violent souls, but only
As the hollow men
The stuffed men.

*****

Notes for **"The Hollow Men"** (cont.)

T.S. Eliot (Thomas Stearns Eliot) (1888~1965) was an American-born English poet, critic and dramatist who was born in St. Louis, Missouri, educated at Harvard, and after 1914 lived in England. He is considered one of the major poets of the twentieth century.

V

Here we go round the prickly pear
Prickly pear prickly pear
Here we go round the prickly pear
At five o'clock in the morning.

Between the idea
And the reality
Between the motion
And the act
Falls the Shadow
                              For Thine is the Kingdom

*****

Between the desire
And the spasm
Between the potency
And the existence
Between the essence
And the descent
Falls the Shadow
                              For thine is the Kingdom

For thine is
Life is
For thine is the

This is the way the world ends
This is the way the world ends
This is the way the world ends
Not with a bang but a whimper.

T.S. Eliot

Notes for
"if everything happens that can't be done"

Read this poem aloud and feel the rhyme invite you both into the poem's rhythm and ultimately its meaning of the unexplainable oneness, if not also the lighthearted play, of two who are one in love. Cleverly, using end-rhyme for the first and last line of each stanza, the author brings the reader further into the author's first parenthetical comment in each stanza on what nature can, yet books cannot, explain. The middle, un-parenthesized line's end-rhyme then finds its twin within the author's second parenthesized comment of the merry and multiplied movement of "we" in each stanza. And while the reader knows one-plus-one is two, the multiplied "one-times-one" becomes the inseparable, between the two, one love of "we."

e.e. cummings (1894~1962) was an American poet and novelist born in Cambridge, Massachusetts. Known for his odd use of typography, punctuation and rhyme to emphasize rhythm, many of his poems make no sense until they are read aloud. He wrote many poems of love and friendship, and this is one of them.

"...we're wonderful one times one"

if everything happens that can't be done

if everything happens that can't be done
(and anything's righter
than books
could plan)
the stupidest teacher will almost guess
(with a run
skip
around we go yes)
there's nothing as something as one

one hasn't a why or because or although
(and buds know better
than books
don't grow)
one's anything old being everything new
(with a what
which
around we go who)
one's every anything so

so world is a leaf is a tree is a bough
(and birds sing sweeter
than books
tell how)
so here is away and so your is a my
(with a down
up
around again fly)
forever was never till now

WHOSE WORDS THESE ARE

now i love you and you love me
(and books are shutter
than books
can be)
and deep in the high that does nothing but fall
(with a shout
each
around we go all)
there's somebody calling who's we

we're everything brighter than even the sun
(we're everything greater
than books
might mean)
we're every anything more than believe
(with a spin
leap
alive we're alive)
we're wonderful one times one

e.e. cummings

Notes for **"[in Just-]"**

Although appearing in many school texts as simply "a lovely poem about spring," this is very complicated poetry. Start with the title: Does "in Just-" mean "as spring starts" or "only in spring;" or does it mean that spring is not just (i.e. unjust)? Why the bracketed title?

What of the never-the-same-positioned, strung-out repetition of the words "far and wee"? What are they intended to mean? What about cummings' famous typology, the poem's 'spatial geography,' which moves the poem from a primarily horizontal reading to a diagonal drift and finally onto a vertical positioning of "far and wee"?

The characters are eddieandbill and bettyandisbel. Why are their names run together? Is it because they are buddies and/or friends? Or, because, as most children do, boys are hanging with boys and girls are hanging with girls?

Then there is another character, "the little lame balloonman," later described as "the queer old balloonman," and then finally a "the goat-footed balloonMan." And what is he doing? He is carrying balloons and he is whistling "far and wee."

And now the action: the whistling sounds and the balloons, of course, will cause eddieandbill and bettyandisbel to look up from the ground where they have been playing marbles and piracies (just like boys) and hop-scotch and jump-rope (just like girls) — enjoying the "mud-luscious" and "puddle-wonderful" (stuff on the ground) world. Do the children follow the balloonman as he passes through the scene? And do they now "come running" and "come dancing," eyes set upward following both the sounds of and what the balloon man holds and the whistling sounds he makes? Certainly, there's spring, or something else, in the air!

e.e. cummings

"...when the world is puddle-wonderful..."

[in Just-]

in Just-
spring   when the world is mud-
luscious the little
lame balloonman

whistles   far   and wee

and eddieandbill come
running from marbles and
piracies and it's
spring

when the world is puddle-wonderful

the queer
old balloonman whistles
far   and   wee
and bettyandisbel come dancing

from hop-scotch and jump-rope and

it's
spring
and
        the
                goat-footed

balloonMan   whistles
far
and wee

e.e. cummings

Notes for **"[in Just-]"** (cont.)

Also, as they are looking up at the balloons and hearing the whistle, do the children note that the balloon man is "little," "lame," "queer," "old" and - finally - (— finally because the adjective is stretched-out with a hyphen) "goat-footed"? Do you think the "balloonman" has matured into a "balloonMan" (capital "M") by the end of the poem? Why? Have all the characters grown up a bit at this point in the poem?

So who is this man with the balloons? Is it the half-man, half-goat god named Pan, the god of fertility, often depicted as old and usually shown whistling, playing on his flute (think here also of the humpbacked, flute-playing, Hopi fertility-deity "Kokopelli")? Notice that the poet does not mention that the balloon man is goat-footed until the very end. Is that for the shock, "Oh my goodness" value?

Is the poem suggesting in spring (the mating season of so many animals and birds) boys and girls of a certain age as well start coming together not to notice, until the last minute, what has unconsciously, but nevertheless powerfully, attracted them to the opposite gender: 'far and **we**'? And is the poet suggesting that there is nothing "unjust" about this rite of spring?

e.e. cummings (1894~1962), born in Cambridge, Massachusetts, was an American poet and novelist who is known for his odd use of typography, punctuation and rhyme to emphasize rhythm. Because of this, many of his poems are best understood when they are read aloud.

WHOSE WORDS THESE ARE

Notes for **"Harlem (2)"**

Written in 1951, this poem, "Harlem (2)," is considered one of Langston Hughes' best short works.

Why is the word "Harlem" included in the poem's title? Consider what five entities a "dream deferred" is compared to, and then note both how the rhyme scheme leads to both a sinking resolution and a powerful ending.

Why the end-line italics, and do these italics symbolize a sort of 'tension' and/or resolve not found in the poem's other lines? What situation and/or who do you think the poet is describing here?

In 1959, using a line from this poem, dramatist Lorraine Hansberry wrote a successful Broadway play *A Raisin in the Sun,* based upon an African-American family's life experiences in the Washington Park Subdivision of Chicago's Woodlawn neighborhood.

Incidentally, Jackson Park, which is located on Woodlawn's east side, includes the site for the Barack Obama Presidential Center, containing the 44th President's library as well.

Langston Hughes (1902~1967), a popular American poet, essayist, novelist, short-story writer, dramatist and journalist, wrote about the African-American experience in the United States. The two volumes of his autobiography are titled *The Big Sea* and *I Wonder as I Wander.* He is thought to be the first African-American to support himself entirely by his writing. "I, too, am America," the closing line of his 1926 poem "I, too," is engraved on the wall of the National Museum of African American History and Culture, dedicated as part of the Smithsonian in Washington, D.C. on September 24, 2016.

"Does it dry up like a raisin in the sun?"

Harlem (2)

What happens to a dream deferred?

Does it dry up
like a raisin in the sun?
Or fester like a sore —
And then run?
Does it stink like rotten meat?
Or crust and sugar over —
like a syrupy sweet?

Maybe it just sags
like a heavy load.

Or does it explode?

Langston Hughes

Notes for
"Do Not Go Gentle Into That Good Night"

Dylan Thomas wrote "Do Not Go Gentle Into That Night" in 1945, when his father was dying. The poet urges his father not to accept death quietly, but to struggle against it until his last breath. Then the poet tells how wise men, good men, wild men, and grave men approach death and concludes by once again addressing his father.

In the second stanza the poet conveys that wise men knowing that death is certain, still fight to live because they believe they have not said all they want to say to influence the world. In the third stanza the poet writes that good men rage against death seeing, after the last wave has passed on a tumultuous bay, how their deeds might have looked on a placid bay. In the fourth stanza Dylan Thomas mentions that wild men fight against death because they realize at the end their busy lives left them no time for anything else. In the fifth stanza the poet says that grave (serious?) men rage against death even though, as their eyes dim, they know they are going to blaze like meteors. Finally, the poet again urges his father to fight against death.

Dylan M. Thomas (October 27, 1914~November 9, 1953), regarded as one of the greatest Welsh poets, was born in Swansea, Wales in 1914 and left school at age sixteen to work as a journalist for a short time. He became well known after the publication of his poem "Light breaks where no sun shines." His most notable poems include "Do Not Go Gentle Into That Good Night" and "And Death Shall Have No Dominion." He also wrote a play *Under Milk Wood* and stories, such as *A Child's Christmas in Wales*.

Although he was a popular poet in the British Isles, Thomas had to supplement his income with reading tours and radio broadcasts. In the 1950s, Thomas went to the United States, where his readings brought him money and made him famous, but his lifelong drinking problem became worse. In New York he became very ill and died on November 9, 1953.

"Do not go gentle into that good night."

Do Not Go Gentle Into That Good Night

Do not go gentle into that good night,
Old age should burn and rave at close of day;
Rage, rage against the dying of the light.

Though wise men at their end know dark is right,
Because their words had forked no lightning they
Do not go gentle into that good night.

Good men, the last wave by, crying how bright
Their frail deeds might have danced in a green bay,
Rage, rage against the dying of the light.

Wild men who caught and sang the sun in flight,
And learn, too late, they grieved it on its way,
Do not go gentle into that good night.

Grave men, near death, who see with blinding sight
Blind eyes could blaze like meteors and be gay,
Rage, rage against the dying of the light.

And you, my father, there on the sad height,
Curse, bless, me now with your fierce tears, I pray.
Do not go gentle into that good night.
Rage, rage against the dying of the light.

Dylan Thomas

Notes for " **The Times They are A-Changin'** "

"The Times They Are a-Changin'" is a song written by Bob Dylan and released on his 1964 album *The Times They Are a-Changin'*. Dylan wrote the song as an attempt to create an anthem of change for a time when the civil rights and folk music movements were closely allied against the backdrop of the Vietnam conflict. Saying it was "a song with a purpose;" based on the Irish and Scottish ballads: 'Come All Ye Bold Highway Men,' and 'Come All Ye Tender Hearted Maidens,' Dylan addresses not only society at large but also takes aim at the social institutions of journalism, politics and family with his warning about the importance of adapting to change.

Ever since its release in 1963, the song "The Times They Are a-Changin'" has influenced many people's views on society, and to some critics the song has biblical overtones. Written as a waltz in three-four time, "The Times They Are a-Changin'" was ranked number fifty-nine on *Rolling Stone*'s 2011 list of the "500 Greatest Songs of All Time," and Dylan's "Like A Rolling Stone" was ranked number one.

In a meeting of United States Poet Laureates at the White House on April 22, 1998, Robert Hass, Rita Dove and Robert Pinsky were asked, "Suppose there's a reading beginning at midnight, 2099. What lines from American poetry of the twentieth century might be recited?" Hass immediately answered, "The Times They Are A-Changin' by Bob Dylan." Rita Dove added, "And that would be very appropriate."

" For the times they are a-changin' "

The Times They Are A-Changin'

Come gather 'round people
Wherever you roam
And admit that the waters
Around you have grown
And accept it that soon
You'll be drenched to the bone
If your time to you is worth savin'
Then you better start swimmin' or you'll sink
      like a stone
For the times they are a-changin'

Come writers and critics
Who prophesize with your pen
And keep your eyes wide
The chance won't come again
And don't speak too soon
For the wheel's still in spin
And there's no tellin' who that it's namin'
For the loser now will be later to win
For the times they are a-changin'

Come senators, congressmen
Please heed the call
Don't stand in the doorway
Don't block up the hall
For he that gets hurt
Will be he who has stalled
There's a battle outside and it is ragin'
It'll soon shake your windows and rattle your walls
For the times they are a-changin'

Notes for **"The Times They are A-Changin' "** (cont.)

Bob Dylan (born **Robert Allen Zimmerman**, May 24, 1941~), an American musician, singer-songwriter, artist, and poet, who performs not only on the guitar — sometimes with a harmonica — but also occasionally on the piano, has been an influential figure in popular music and culture for more than six decades. In the 1960s his early songs, such as "Blowin' in the Wind," "Masters of War," "A Hard Rain's Gonna Fall," and the ironic "With God on Our Side," became anthems for the civil rights and anti-war movements.

Bob Dylan, as he has continually done throughout his career, reinvented himself and transitioned from the folk music scene in 1965 with his six-minute, hard-driving, rock single "Like a Rolling Stone," and since then he has written in many American song traditions — from blues to country to reggae to rock-and-roll and even jazz. He still returns to all these genres, including folk music, forever innovating in the studio and during his seemingly neverending, annual tours. Bob Dylan's album, *Shadows in the Night*, released in early February, 2014, includes several songs associated with Frank Sinatra, as does both his 2016 album *Fallen Angels* and his latest, three-CD set entitled *Triplicate*.

He has received Grammy, Golden Globe, and Academy Awards; has been inducted into the Rock and Roll Hall of Fame, and won a Pulitzer Prize in 2008 for "his profound impact on popular music and American culture, marked by lyrical compositions of extraordinary poetic power." In May 2012, Dylan received the Presidential Medal of Freedom from President Barack Obama. Having written hundreds of songs, with unique phrasing and poignant, purposeful lyrics, some people consider Bob Dylan to be "the Shakespeare of our time." On October 13th, 2016, Bob Dylan was awarded the Nobel Prize in Literature.

Come mothers and fathers
Throughout the land
And don't criticize
What you can't understand
Your sons and your daughters
Are beyond your command
Your old road is rapidly agin'
Please get out of the new one if you can't lend
       your hand
For the times they are a-changin'

The line it is drawn
The curse it is cast
The slow one now
Will later be fast
As the present now
Will later be past
The order is rapidly fadin'
And the first one now will later be last
For the times they are a-changin'

Bob Dylan

WHOSE WORDS THESE ARE

About the Compilers and Commentators

John J. Dilenschneider, B.A. University of Notre Dame, M.A. The Ohio State University, J.D. Northwestern University, is a former corporate attorney and U.S. Bankruptcy Judge, who taught at The Ohio State University in its English Department and in its School of Law.

j. Justin Dilenschneider, B.A. University of Notre Dame; M.A. The University of Montana, has over twenty-five years of experience in English education at the secondary and tertiary levels, holding assistant and associate professorships at Toyo University, The University of KitaKyushu, and Hitotsubashi University's Graduate School of Commerce and Management, where he implemented, managed, and taught within a comprehensive, communicative English curriculum for the undergraduate Faculty of Commerce and Management. He now teaches English communication skills and conducts research at Hakodate University in Hokkaido, Japan.

ACKNOWLEDGEMENTS

We would like to acknowledge the help, advice and support of our families and friends, counsel and logistics from Dilenschneider Group International, cover-design expertise from Jaye Medalia, and in particular, the patient assistance of our editor Jim Zebora at Significance Press.

WHOSE WORDS THESE ARE

CPSIA information can be obtained
at www.ICGtesting.com
Printed in the USA
LVOW11s0624181217
560141LV00001B/153/P

9 780998 528915